iAware:

Becoming Self-Aware
&
College Bound

by Robert Pasick, Ph.D.
Lauryn Humphreys and Ali Houmani

Copyright and Contact Info

For more information, including videos and other resources, visit RobPasick.com

Copyright © 2018 Robert Pasick, Ph.D.
All Rights Reserved.

You may contact the authors at rob@leadersconnect.com

Table of Contents art work by Rachelle Viola

Preface

As a Harvard trained Psychologist with over 45 years of experience, my passion is to help people increase their self-awareness in order take control of their lives and create goals for their future. I have written several books on the topic and also teach a class at the University of Michigan Ross School of Business. In the Spring of 2018, my associate, Beth, and I began discussing how my materials could be more applicable to teenagers, especially before they **begin** the college application process. That summer, as luck would have it, I was approached separately by two very exceptional high school students, Lauryn Humphreys and Ali Houmani, who wanted to do an internship for me. They were familiar with my work in emotional intelligence, and both stated they wished that they had similar curriculum offered in their high schools. Hence, a project was conceived. Ali and Lauryn read through my current book, *Self Aware: A Guide for Success in Work and Life*, and completed the weekly assignments. Beth and I would meet with them regularly to discuss what they had learned and then to also re-write or add chapters that were more applicable to what they, as high school students, were experiencing. These very motivated students researched the topic of self-awareness and also sought advice from their peers, parents, and young adults currently enrolled at the University of Michigan. At the end of the process they held forums at local high schools with the target population. The forum would review the book and give feedback. The end result is this book, *iAware: Becoming Self Aware and College Bound* which will help you, the reader, to become more aware of yourself and what you want out of life.

You are about to embark on a journey of self- discovery that will help you in the process of choosing the right college for you, writing strong essays about yourself, and giving great interviews. It is our hope that this book will become a well-worn companion for you, through your ages and stages. As you grow and enter into new life experiences and challenges, you may need to revisit some chapters of this book. You will be surprised to learn that based on your circumstances the chapters will take on new meaning to you. Self-Awareness is a continual process, but it is well worth the investment.

Book Overview

You might think about this book as a workbook. In addition to stories, it includes questions and exercises designed to help you better understand yourself. It contains thirteen chapters in three parts.

Part One is *"Why This Book?"*

- Chapter 1: Overview of the book
- Chapter 2: Current Life Challenges
- Chapter 3: Why is Emotional Intelligence Crucial to Your Passage into Increased Independence

Part Two: Understanding Who You Are

- Chapter 4: Self-Discovery Step One: Discover Your Strengths.
- Chapter 5: Self-Discovery Step Two: Define Your Interests and Passions
- Chapter 6: Self-Discovery Step Three: Understand Your Personality
- Chapter 7: Self-Discovery Step Four: Manage Your Energy and Your Body.
- Chapter 8: Self-Discovery Step Six: Manage Your Mind.
- Chapter 9: Self-Discovery Step Seven: Invest in Your Relationships.

Part Three asks you to "put it all together, to find your collegiate sweet spot"

- Chapter 10: Define Your Mission and Values
- Chapter 11: Map Your Lifestyle Values
- Chapter 12: Define Your Purpose/Setting Goals
- Chapter 13: Personal Development Plan and "Graduation".

This book contains summaries of research, personal stories and voices from Dr Rob, Ali, and Lauryn, as well as their peers and Dr. Rob's clients and students.

Some chapter sections and assignments link out to online resources such as assessments, articles, and videos. We will maintain a list of resources for the book on robpasick.com. We have done our best to make sure that these links work at the time of publication, but the links may stop working at any time due to changes on third-party sites. We have also included worksheets in the appendices section near the back of the book. Also, those reading this book on a dedicated e-reader (such Kindle) may not have a good experience visiting these websites from their e-reader. Instead, they may prefer visiting the resources on a different device. Please visit robpasick.com for the most up-to-date information and resource list.

Daily Journaling/Reflections/Assignments

Daily Journaling

To receive the most benefit from this book and your journey to becoming more self-aware, we recommend daily journaling. We have included journal pages in the appendix section in the back of this book. There are enough pages for 30 days of journaling. Feel free to make copies of the journal pages

Your Reflections

Many of the topics are followed by reflection questions, "Your Reflections." The reflection questions are meant to be thought-starters. Not all reflection questions will apply to you, so feel free to choose reflections while challenging yourself.

Your Assignment

> For most topics, you'll also have an assignment, "Your Assignment." It will look like this section!
>
> You will benefit from the assignments, so make the time to invest in your personal growth.
>
> Many assignments will go into your Personal Development Plan, which is an appendix in the back of this book. It will give you a working document for continued goal-setting and reflection. You may download our Personal Development plan template as a Google doc online. You will need to copy the document so that you can edit and customize your plan.
>
> Enjoy the process!

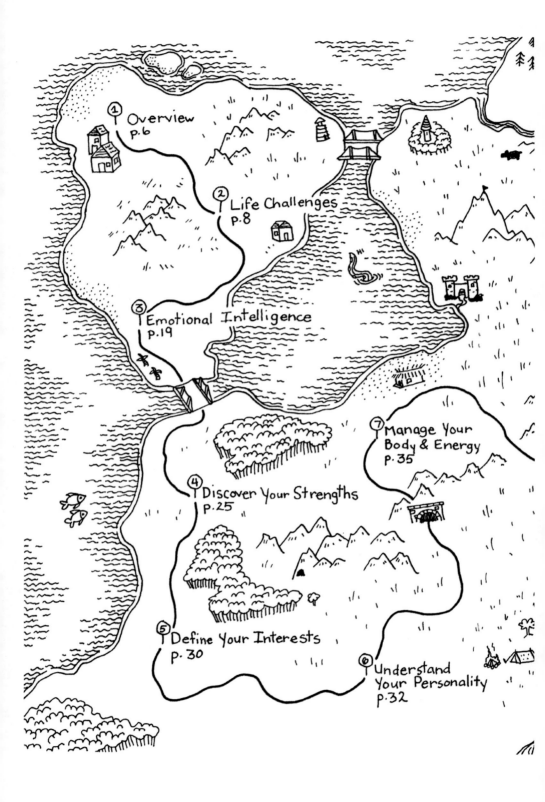

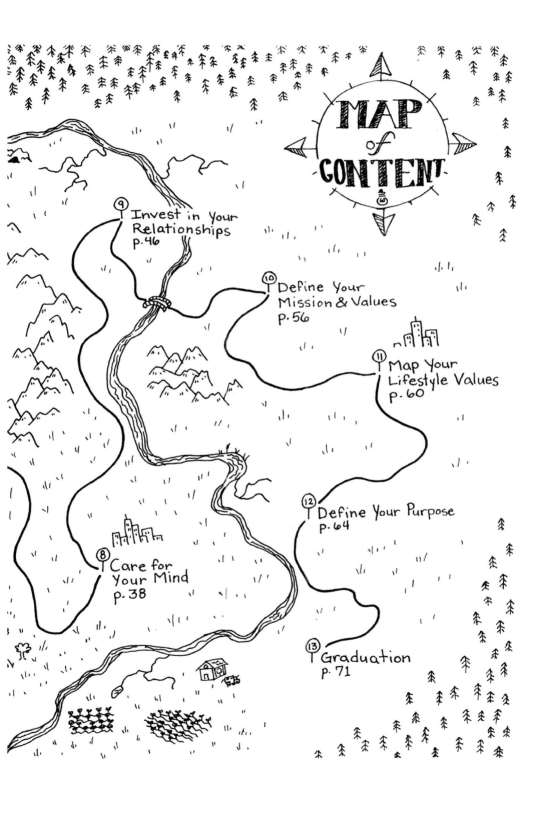

Chapter 1: Overview of This Book

This book is designed to take you through a series of exercises that will lead you on a path of self-discovery toward increased emotional intelligence. By reading and completing the exercises you will:
- Gain a better sense of self-awareness.
- Develop your emotional intelligence competency
- Craft a personal vision for success in college and career.
- Plan how to create a team of resources to help you in the pursuit of your college goals.

Why should you read this book?

Understanding yourself is the key to choosing a college that is right for you. When you are able to fully understand your strengths, your blind spots, and your passions, you will be more likely to identify what you want out of a college.

Gaining a better understanding of self also enables you to write the very best college essay to increase your chances of getting into your choice college. College and university admissions offices could not possibly meet and interview every applicant. Even if they are able to interview you, they are only getting a small glimpse into who you are. When you become self-aware, you will be able to compose a meaningful essay that gives the reader a sense that they truly learned more about you.

Reasons to Read This Book

Reason one: You are in high school, especially a junior or senior, and everyone is asking where you are going to college. This sounds like an easy question to answer but it's not for so many reasons:
- A. Will you be able to get into the college of your choice?
- B. Have you considered all of your college options?
- C. Are you aware of funding resources that are available?
- D. Is it the right fit for you?
- E. Do you know what major you choose?
- F. Have you thought about the careers/majors that may not exist but could emerge in the next few years?
- G. Do you even want or need to go to college?

Reason Two: You are ready to really think about how to answer these questions and also explore more about yourself.
  A. At this age. it's hard to know you where you want to go in life, let alone where you want to go to college and what you want to study.
  B. Without knowing yourself, you may be easily swayed by others' opinions about where you should go, what you should major in, and your perceived limitations.
  C. You may be torn by thinking you have to know exactly, at this moment, what career is right for you. Yet, keep in mind, you need to take time to explore yourself. For example:
      a. What are your **Strengths**?
      b. What are you **Passionate** about?
      c. What is your **Personality**?
      d. How do you manage **Relationships**?

Reason Three: You are considering what kind of college is right for you. This takes in many factors:
  A. Location
      a. How close to or far away from home do you want to be?
      b. Do you prefer an urban, city or small-town setting?
      c. Does climate matter to you?
  B. Cost
      a. Can you qualify for financial aid or scholarships?
      b. Can you afford out of state tuition or do you need to stay in state?
      c. Can you afford the tuition of a private college or do you need to only consider public institutions?
      d. Will you receive financial assistance from your family or will you need to work and/or get loans to pay for college?
  C. Size
      a. Extracurricular activities
          i. If you like sports, does the college have a good team for you to follow or to join
      b. Arts and Entertainment

Reason Four: You are seeking a competitive edge in choosing the college that's right for you, and ultimately developing skills to increase your chances of future success.

Chapter 2: Current Life Challenges:

Every stage of life presents challenges that we must either learn to adapt to or master. As a psychologist and two high school seniors, we are hearing more and more that kids are facing extreme pressure to not only perform well, but to exceed in every aspect of their life that is important to them, such as academics, sports, music, or arts. More young kids and teenagers today are being diagnosed with anxiety and depression than they were twenty years ago. In fact, the World Health Organization (WHO) recently released a September 2018 report stating that one in three college students worldwide have a mental health condition. This statistic appears to be trending up.

We want you to be aware that even though it is important to succeed, it is not worth it to succeed at any cost. Your mental health is very important to your future success. Take care of yourself. Practice the following self-care:

- Stay focused
- Do your best, but don't "should yourself" into a frenzy. (We will talk later in this book about the concept of "shoulding" yourself but for now it means exactly what it sounds like.)
- Take time to breathe and relax
- Give yourself positive self-reflections, and trust that things will work out. If one door closes the second door may be better for you anyway
- Seek a friend, relative, or a counselor if you feel like you cannot manage the pressures you are facing at this time.

Here are a few life challenges (there's sure to be more) that high schoolers may be dealing with:
1. Maintaining their GPA
2. Taking ACT/SAT
3. Decisions:
    a. How to spend free time with friends and activities
        i. Managing "FOMO" - Fear of Missing Out
    b. Deciding which classes to take in high school
    c. Deciding the career you want to pursue
4. Comfort with decisions
5. College criteria -meeting a particular college's acceptance criteria
6. Leaving their comfort zone
7. Other life responsibilities (family responsibilities, athletics, clubs, friends, jobs)

Chapter 2

How to Cope with Life Challenges:

We interviewed forty-two college students to gain a better perspective on how they successfully coped with their personal struggles in high school. These students were from diverse backgrounds and in different stages of their college careers. Though seemingly very different, they still shared a common thread of life concerns and how they overcome them by planning, performing gut checks, and seeking advice.

Dear Younger Me

A couple of students shared with us a letter to their seventeen-year-old selves to help us gain perspective on what they thought was important at that time in their lives and compare it to what ultimately mattered in their lives. Read these powerful letters below:

Letter 1:

Dear Younger Me:

Relax! I completely understand that you're probably feeling really stressed about choosing a college, trying to get into the best programs possible, and discover yourself. However, you're going to end up changing your mind after first semester of university and I'm willing to bet on it. Actually, I feel like you should be even more open to making different decisions on your career path and pick what you find interesting most. I know at this point you have a whole strategy mapped out about becoming a doctor and exploring your interests in business – and although you did end up sticking to that plan, there are many points in my university career where I wish I would have done something else. The "plan" that you have provides comfort – however, it takes way too much to commit to it and at the same time explore other options and do everything effectively. My greatest advice, pick what you want and don't care what anyone else says or thinks.

Another key advice I'd provide to you, do not hesitate to get mental health support. You will continuously refuse to maintain what you thought at the time as "Masculinity" but it's just not worth it because your career will suffer.

We're not that much different – sure I'm more mature, intelligent, and wise relative to you, however, with respect to character you're not too different than when you started. Meet as many people as you can who are different than yourself to learn as much as you can and explore everything as much as you possible can.
Good Luck, Alex

Letter 2:

Dear Younger Me":

There are four things you need to know. 1. Where you go to college will not significantly alter your future success. 2. Many students at the most elite colleges transfer out. 3. If you have a dream school, you must express interest and reach out. 4. Go to a college where you fit in and can be yourself.

The first and second points go together. No matter where you go to college, if you work extremely hard studying, engaging in meaningful activities, and continuously learning, you will land in the right place. Yes, a college with a good brand name can help, but it won't be the difference between success and failure. On the flip side, it's sometimes a blessing for students to not get accepted into their "dream schools," because the homework and lifestyle would have been too much. It is truly shocking how many students transfer out of top schools. The third point is the reason why most of my college friends got in. If you don't engage with the admissions counselors, visit the college campus, write an incredibly thoughtful and well-tailored college essay, it becomes infinitely harder to get into a particular college. Expressing relentless interest in a school is a must. Fourth, I went to a school where I could be myself, from the clubs I joined on campus to the students I became best friends with. If a college doesn't feel right when you step on campus, and if it doesn't match your vision of college, it may not be the right place, and that is fine. Don't stress about getting into the perfect school, as all schools have their pros and cons, and enjoy one of the best years of your life.

Jonny

From these letters, we learned that ***it is okay to not know exactly what you are going to do.*** As high schoolers we sometimes feel that we have to have our whole life mapped out. We feel like we are defined by the choices we will make for our futures, and regardless of the circumstances, we must stick to our original plans.

Alex told his younger self to stop putting so many implications and expectations on himself that he **had to** become a doctor. Alex learned that his passion was dynamic, not static, and that plans can change. According to Alex, the college you choose is not as important as the effort you will put into it once you get there. He learned to focus more on his passions versus what others think or expect of him. Alex also let us know that it was okay to honestly represent yourself, even if it included what others may see as a deficit, like mental health problems. Overall, Alex encourages us to follow our passions, know that we will grow and change, and also to accept and take care of ourselves.

Jonny gave his younger self advice to reach out to college admissions counselors and ensure that they know how interested he is that college. He advised to visit college campuses, and if it doesn't meet your vision of the college, it may not be the right fit. Stay open minded though because even though you may not get into your "dream college" it may not have turned out to be right for you. Overall, college is what you make it. Be active, make friends, and join clubs. Most importantly, don't be afraid of rejection. Keep taking risks. They eventually pay off.

What We Want to Know from College Students' Experience

We also had many great responses to a questionnaire we developed to gain better insight on what college students have learned about their self-awareness, their decisions, their coping skills and how they adapted to college life:

1. **How self-aware were you as a high school junior, and how self-aware are you now?**

    I have always been self-aware, but the number and variety of experiences in college have made me infinitely more self-aware – from dance classes to parties to living with roommates. ~Jonny

    I was not self-aware at all as a junior in high school. I did not know how to adapt my communication style to others. I was still figuring out who I was and was more internal through my high school years. I really learned in college how my actions affect other people. Softball taught me to manage my emotions and recognize warning signs in my self talk and mood. ~Taylor

    I've always been a reflective person and I've always understood my ambition, however, the older I get the more I hone in on to these different characteristics and focus on trying to bring out the best of myself in them. ~Alex.

    Frankly, I wasn't so self-aware as a junior with what type of occupation would be a good fit for me. It's hard to know that a particular job isn't what's right for you when you haven't gotten real exposure to it. While working as a wealth management summer analyst for JPM, I finally got that real-life exposure to come to my senses that the role was not something I'd want to do long term. Having to work from 7-7pm every day, also influenced me to be more mindful of the fact that I need to be more careful in the careers I pursue. I would highly encourage others to speak to others who've gone down the career paths they are currently following or considering following. Better yet, shadowing would give an even greater opportunity for developing self-awareness in your career interests. ~Ila

2. **How did you prepare for applying to colleges?**

Research, research, research and research. I applied to and visited schools I thought I had a good shot with, got into Michigan, and that was that. ~Jonny G.

I didn't really prepare much. I filled out the college applications looking to see where would take me and went forward from there. Financing was always more of an issue on my mind so factoring in cost would definitely be a factor in applying to universities. ~Alex

I didn't plan on studying out of state because my parents wanted me to stay at home. So, when figuring out which colleges to apply to, I only focused on those in Michigan. All through high school I kept my GPA up and took challenging courses that I thought admissions would like to see in a student to prove they can handle challenging coursework.
I also took the ACTs. Retrospectively, I wish I'd taken the SATs because they focused on subject areas, I was better in. I'd recommend considering your strengths and being thoughtful about which test is a best match with what you bring to the table.
Finally, I began the essay portion of my application in September and worked with one of my teachers to craft and revise them so that I could send them in by the early admission deadline if one existed. I wish I had started thinking through my application earlier in August when I wasn't as busy with semester classes. ~Ila

3. **What made you choose Michigan?**

I chose Michigan because it was the only school, I visited where I felt magic in the air and could see myself growing and thriving. ~ Jonny G.

I had two choices in front of me when applying to colleges – Michigan and Berkeley. I ended up choosing Michigan because it's closer to home (Detroit). Not only that, programs weren't necessarily that different and Berkeley was just much more expensive relative to Michigan. ~Alex

As a kid, I attended the cultural shows put on by the University of Michigan Persian Student Association. As silly as it sounds, that's what piqued my interest in attending the University. As I got older, I learned about how much resources and opportunities are available at Michigan. I would find academic rigor and develop connections with other bright minds. Finally, I love the small-town vibe that the campus has, and that there are so many ways to get involved on campus. ~Ila

4. **How did you adjust to college? Was is what you thought it was going to be?**

    In terms of making friends and learning, college was what I thought it was going to be. I was prepared well for my classes, and I eventually made the right friends. However, my first semester I was rejected from at least fifteen clubs on campus, and it very stressful and upsetting. The way I adjusted was that I founded my own club and made it completely inclusive so that anyone could join. It is currently thriving and has made the campus a better place, and I am proud. ~Jonny

    It was difficult at first to go from being in an environment where you knew everyone and had a lot of friends to starting a journey where you knew no one and no one knew you. FOMO (Fear of missing out) will definitely hit you but let it hit and slide because it'll continuously take hold of you if you don't address that it exists and why it exists. ~Alex

    I had an easy adjustment to college. I attended a dual enrollment program that allowed me to take college classes while taking classes in high school. I think the biggest change in college was the autonomy that I had. I made decisions about how much I'd study, the extracurriculars I'd be involved in, my major, the classes I'd be taking, and how much fun I'd have over the weekends by myself.
    I thought college course at the University of Michigan would be very challenging, but I realized with strategic planning and a disciplined mindset, it could all be manageable. ~Ila

5. **Did you face any challenges along the way? If so, how did you handle them?**

    Softball was always a major challenge, physically, mentally, emotionally. It is draining to have 3 games and 3 finals in the same week. The adversity the sport brings is even more difficult. I didn't play as much as I wanted to and it was hard to approach my coach. We got along, but we just had different personalities and communication styles. I talked a little bit about this, but I learned to adjust my leadership and communication style to please her and still be a leader and impact player on the team. My experience was significantly better once I learned to do this. I felt like she was on my side. ~Taylor S.

    The largest difficulty I've faced along the way would be adjusting to college life. Moving away is difficult, but after a few weeks I got used to living alone. Mistakes are made on what to eat, who to hang out with, when to do your homework and study for exams, and how to live in general, but eventually everyone figures it out. ~Alex

    As a transfer student, I did find it more difficult to develop strong friendships on campus since everyone had already formed their friendship circles. Joining

Chapter 2

organizations helped but only to an extent, and I found everybody herded up with those that were similar to each other in their appearances, values, and what they had in common. Attending Ross, I didn't find too many individuals with similar connections with me. I had to push myself to break out my comfort zone and get to know people that I didn't have strong commonalities with. This has helped me work more comfortably with a greater diversity of people.

Avoiding the distractions when being on campus and living on campus can also be challenge. You have to really define your goals and put them first at all costs to succeed. ~Ila

6. **Did you change your mind at any point in the application process or during college?**

I was incredibly close to transferring out of Michigan – it was too large and overwhelming, the winter was freezing, and the extracurricular clubs were too exclusive. In the end, however, I was convinced to stay by my college friends who wanted to share the college experience (the good and bad), and reminded me that "Those who stay will be champions." ~Jonny

I changed my major during college. I didn't think I was smart enough to get into Ross. If I could tell my younger self anything, it would be to be confident in everything. Most of life and success is due to attitude. ~Taylor

Personally, I didn't change my mind at all throughout the application process but I did spend a lot of time trying to decide what I wanted to do during college and what my "plan" told me to do. In the end, my best advice would be to do what excites you and you would enjoy pulling three all-nighters in a row for. ~Alex

Of course. There will be times where we all feel intimidated and question our abilities in our classes or rethink if our major is the right one for us. Prior to college, I believed I was average at everything and didn't have a particular strength in one subject over another. After taking the time for self-reflection and really breaking down what I've enjoyed doing as a child. Also, while those who are older than you will try to give you advice about what to do with your future, take their advice with caution - they could be just as lost as you and their values/interests likely differ as well. ~Ila

Thoughts from Lauryn:

After hearing these student responses, I felt incredibly encouraged. The college students shared that **"yes"**, they have failed. However, they have grown from their failures and turned them into successes. An example of growth can

> be seen in Jonny. He did not let club denial define him, but rather created his own club. I feel like we can ultimately learn that the road to success is not clearly defined, and everyone fails at some point along the way.
>
> Another point I found intriguing is why each student chose the University of Michigan opposed to other schools. One respondent talked about the vibes he got when stepping on campus, and another talked about programs and pricing. The last shared that she chose Michigan because of experiences she had at the University while growing up. From these responses, we gained a deeper understanding that no one can choose a college for YOU except for YOU. There isn't a right or a wrong way to choose a school, and everyone should figure out what way is best for them.

What is FOMO?

So far, FOMO (fear of missing out) has been mentioned several times. FOMO is defined as anxiety that an exciting or interesting event may currently be happening elsewhere, often aroused by posts seen on a social media website. One student shared her experiences with FOMO and steps she took to overcome it.

> What I would like to share with you is how I've learned throughout college to manage FOMO. The fear of missing out, FOMO, frequently drove a lot of my actions as an underclassman. I would definitely do things that I thought other people thought were "cool" things to do, and post things on my social media to show off these things. If I didn't go to a party one night, I would watch snapchat stories and go on Instagram to keep up with what everyone else was doing, often feeling bad and guilty for not doing what they were. Even if I stayed in to do homework, I typically wouldn't be able to focus because I felt jealous of my other friends that were all together having a good time while I felt like I was being lame at home. I know this was most prevalent my freshman year, when I was still figuring out who my real friends at college were, still trying to make a name for myself here.
>
> Now, as a senior, I realize how much less I experience FOMO. I no longer feel guilty about not going out on a night that all of my friends are, even when they snapchat me and text me specifically telling me to come out with them while they're there. During fall break, as I spent time with my family and friends that are around, even though I always checked my phone and social medias, I had no jealousy of any of

my friends that went on a trip. I honestly was very excited and happy for them that they had a fun break, but I am also very happy with the way I spent my own break.

Each of our priorities are different, and happiness comes in many, many forms. I've come to a place where, rather than experience FOMO, I am instead recognizing that there are so many different experiences to have, and there will always be something to be a part of, but I need to pick and choose what experiences I want to have at what point in my life.

I think that if I ever begin to experience FOMO in the future, there are key questions I will need to ask myself of.

1. **Where is the FOMO stemming from? Is there something you're insecure about, like the quantity or quality of your friendships that is manifesting through FOMO?**
2. **What are your priorities? Is this experience so critical to your life path right now? Or will there be other times to pursue this opportunity?**
3. **Are you happy with what you're doing otherwise? Without needing to broadcast what you're doing to the world?**

I am very glad I've made this mature growth in my life thus far to recognize these things, while being able to recognize healthy ways to assess the situation and fix my mood. ~Wendy

If you at all are aware of social media, you have probably experienced FOMO at one time or another. Wendy's three-part advice to manage FOMO is very sound, and can help you choose which life experiences you want to enjoy for personal reasons rather than because of a fear of missing out.

One Piece of Advice

Finally, we took advantage of having so many college students willing to give high school juniors and seniors advice, that we asked them to share one piece of advice about their college experience. Below are some of the responses about what they wished they would have done during their college years:

> Talk to that one person you thought you would have never talked to. You can learn so much about a person and you have no idea what value they can bring. ~Avanika

Chapter 2

> *As a freshman in college, you are working so hard to find your place that you end up creating this bubble around yourself. Explore communities and activities early on in college. ~Arathi*

> *In college there is a lot of pressure to know what you want to do after you graduate, and I think it is important to know it's okay to not know exactly what your future holds. Instead, you should try different things so you can carve a path for yourself rather than having it forced upon you. ~Jillian G.*

> *In our college majors we can get very comparative and compare ourselves to what other people are accomplishing. It is important to follow you own passion and not let other people's trajectories put pressure on you to pursue something that is not right for you. ~Alisha*

> *Don't let your failures hold you back. I did not get accepted into my college of choice and I felt like a failure. I was also very mad. I went into college with a negative mindset. My advice to you is to make the best of it and work hard to develop your path in the college that you attend. Now, I am so glad that I attended my college and I couldn't imagine I would have had any better experience anywhere else. I wish I hadn't wasted time being feeling rejected and just focused on getting the most from my college experience early on. ~ Jillian W.*

> *Don't be afraid to go out of your comfort zone and try to better yourself. You can't be afraid to fail. Also, be aware that people have preconceived notions and may label you a failure before they even know what you are capable of. Don't be afraid of these people, and don't avoid situations where you may prove them right because you very well may prove them wrong. ~Devin*

They also gave us advice about friendships and social experiences:

> *From the athletic perspective, many of us don't get outside of the bubble of our sport. Even though I always know I have my team and they have my back, I have been trying to broaden my friendships to include those outside of my sport. I have found that this opens me up to new experiences I would not have otherwise had and has introduced me to so many new friendship opportunities. ~Kim*

> *Even if you are not making friends with everyone in your class, you should always carry yourself well and treat everyone with respect. You never know down the road who will end up being in your community, an acquaintance of an acquaintance, or someone who will be able to help you in your career. Beyond being friends, it is important to develop positive relationship where people have a good feeling about you. ~Mel*

Chapter 2

We were very fortunate to receive such tremendous support and advice from the college students. We included most of the information they shared with us because we believe every nugget of it is worthy. It is our hope that some of this advice will help you either in your college decision, your interactions with others, or your future college career.

Summary Assignment for Current Life Challenges

Write down your current life challenges in the first column of the chart below. Put an *X* in the column indicating if the challenge is in your control or out of your control. Prioritize the ones that are in your control. Write at least one action you can take for the challenges that are in your control.

Current Life Challenge	In Your Control?	Out of Your Control?	Priority (1 being greatest)	Action Plan

Imagine yourself five years from now. Write a few paragraphs, or short story, about your future self. Now imagine that future self-writing a letter to your high school self. What would it say?

Chapter 3: Why is Emotional Intelligence Crucial to You:

The Key to Self-Understanding and Decision Making

Thoughts From Lauryn:

Before discovering the core principles of self- awareness, I felt that I had a firm grasp in the area. This turned out to be, for the most part, untrue. My junior year of high school, I took a class on the subject. I liked the principles, but felt some of the practices were difficult to maintain. For example, meditation. I drifted away from discovering my personal self-awareness because I felt that I had to meditate and had to write down my daily thoughts in order to be fully self-aware.

Principles of Self Awareness

Here are the core principles of this book:

- **Self-awareness is step number one and the cornerstone of emotional intelligence.** Without adequate self-awareness, we struggle to understand others, to manage ourselves, and to develop healthy relationships.
- **Self-awareness is a process.** Because the world around us is engaged in continuous change, and because we are forever changing, we never finish developing our own sense of self-awareness.
- **Self-awareness is never wholly about the self.** We mostly learn about ourselves in relation to others.
- **No one succeeds alone.** All major accomplishments occur within a system of cooperation and competition.
- **To learn who we are, we have to act upon the world by trying things.** We learn by action, by making mistakes, and by learning from these mistakes. We cannot become self-aware solely through self-reflection. We must act upon our world to learn from it.

A good, successful life begins with self-awareness.

The Emotional Intelligence Competencies

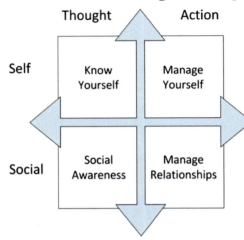

Emotional Intelligence competencies can be thought of as a grid of four squares. In this grid, the self is on top and your social interactions are below.

On the right are the thinking competencies: know yourself, be aware of others. On the left are action competencies: manage yourself and manage relationships.

Self-Awareness is the Key to Success

Know Thyself.
-Socrates

Sages throughout history and across cultures have urged us to be self-aware, and thereby understand our world. Modern psychological sciences have consistently reinforced the idea that well-being begins with self-awareness.

One key example of this insight comes from modern psychological research dedicated to emotional intelligence. Beginning with Professor David McClelland, for whom Dr. Rob was a teaching assistant at Harvard University, and continuing through the research of his classmates, Daniel Goleman and Rick Boyatzis, it has been shown that **self-awareness is the cornerstone of emotional intelligence**. In order to understand other people, we must first understand ourselves. In order to manage any relationship, we must possess self-awareness and other awareness. In order to manage our emotions, we must first understand ourselves. And to manage the complexity of complicated relationships, such as those we find in family, school, teams or work, we must first understand ourselves in relationship to others.

Key Questions to Ask Yourself on Emotional Intelligence (EI)

Here are some questions to ask yourself about your level of emotional intelligence. For each set of questions, there are a few options to increase your competence.

How well do I know myself?

- What are my **strengths**?
- What are my core **values**?
- What is my **purpose**?
- What are my **passions** and **interests**?
- What are my **blind spots**?
- What are the **keys to my personality**?

To enhance self-awareness
- Practice some form of self-reflection:
    - meditate or pray
    - write about your feelings
    - talk others about your feelings and listen, really listen, to their feedback.
- Set goals: know what you want and where you want to go.

How well do I understand others?

- Do I **know** how others feel?
- Can I **feel** how others feel?
- How well do I **seek to understand** others?
- How well do I **read** individual differences?
- How **sensitive** am I to the feelings of others?
- How well do I **understand myself** in relation to others?

To enhance empathy
- **Practice active listening:** not debating, not defending, and not counter-attacking.
- **Seek first to understand** rather than to be understood.

How well do I manage my emotions and my actions?

- How well do I **handle stress**?
- How well do I **manage anger**?
- Do I know what I "**say to myself**" about difficult situations?
- Can I **talk myself down** from getting upset?
- Can I **manage my moods**?
- Do I know how to get myself **out of a bad mood**?

- How well do I **manage my time**?
- How well do I **take care of myself** (mind and body)?

To enhance self-management
- Be aware of **emotional flooding**: the moment your emotions trump your ability to think.
- Be aware of **faulty thinking**. Bad ideas can lead to bad action. Example bad ideas include: I must be right all the time. I must never admit vulnerability. I must be loved and approved of by everybody, all the time.
- Avoid **counter-attacking**.
- Practice **delaying gratification**.

How well do I display empathy toward others?

- How well are you able to **express your feelings**?
- How **positive** are you with others?
- How well do you exercise good **self-restraint** when dealing with difficult situations?
- Personal and professional **elevator pitch**: How do I introduce myself to people I meet?
- How are you at **asking good questions** of others?
- How well do you **actively listen** to the answers?
- How are you at **sustaining long-term relationships** (family, social, personal)?
- How would you rate your ability to **influence others**?
- How would you rate your ability to **lead others**?

To manage relationships
- Know it's **not always about you**.
- Realize we are all **on key personality spectra** and may need different amounts of time or rationale for decisions.

Emotional Intelligence: An Example

Emotional intelligence is the best predictor of long-term success in life.
Research has shown that emotional intelligence is the key factor in the ability of individuals to get along well in relationships. Generations will see this play out in the span of their lives: emotional intelligence is valued even more than intellectual intelligence and technical skills.

Many leaders tend to be competitive, hard-driving people. They have high IQs, but sometimes their emotional intelligence lags far behind.

Recently, we sat down with Taylor, a Division One college softball player who was also completing her bachelor's degree in Accounting at the University of Michigan Ross School of Business. Taylor shared stories about her experience as a student athlete.

College athletes come from diverse backgrounds each responding differently to various coaching styles. As you can imagine, each teammate was a top tier college athlete, each being extremely successful in their high school athletic careers. They not only need to learn to manage themselves in the college environment but also to form relationships with team members.

As an upperclassman on the softball team, Taylor encountered a freshman player who struggled finding her comfort zone and where she fit in on this prestigious team. Being an empathetic leader, Taylor noticed the signs of this player's struggle. Taylor's first goal was to build a rapport with this player. She went out of her way to talk to her in a kind and welcoming manner. The player responded positively to Taylor's efforts, and as a result started to develop comradery with others on the team. As she felt more comfortable with other players, she began to take more risks to show them her athletic ability. Because of Taylor's focus on inclusivity, this player is one of the more successful players on the team.

Taylor was more comfortable with the leadership style described above: compassionate and patient. Halfway through her collegiate softball career, Taylor was designated as the captain of the team. Once Taylor assumed the role of captain, her coach expected a much stricter leadership style from her. At first, Taylor didn't believe that certain leadership style (being strict, yelling, etc.) at her teammates was the best way to reach the team's goals and develop team success. To combat this dilemma, Taylor took her natural leadership tendencies and combined them with what the coach wanted. She kept her teammates accountable and took a no-nonsense attitude about certain things, but also made sure to take a personal interest to help facilitate team chemistry and confidence. Consequently, she realized she could continue to maintain her previous leadership attributes while pleasing her coach. She maintained her kind-hearted mannerisms while making sure everyone was on top of their role as an athlete and teammate.

From Taylor's experiences, we learned that being an emotionally intelligent leader is being an adaptive leader. Her past struggles show us that you must get to know the needs of those you lead while also being aware of the expectations of your superiors.

What to do to improve emotional intelligence:
- **Keep a mood log**. Several times a day, write down how you are feeling. Look back at the end of the week and assess how tuned in you were to your own emotions. Look for patterns.
- **Avoid shaming others**. It can be highly destructive. You may be aware that shaming is destructive to others; you must be aware that shaming is destructive to your reputation.
- At school or at home, **make a point of empathizing with others**. Put yourself in that person's shoes. Think about what it would feel like to be that person.

- If you're having a dispute, **look at it from the other person's viewpoint**. Try writing out a narrative of the disagreement from the other person's standpoint.

> **Thoughts From Lauryn:**
> After studying self-awareness with Dr. Rob and talking with Taylor, I learned that self-awareness is not always rituals and journaling, but is more about knowing yourself. When you are comfortable with yourself and your actions, you are practicing self-awareness. I think as high schoolers, we think that everything we do needs to be logical and uniform. Self-awareness is different for everyone.
>
> After learning self-awareness, I felt much less stressed than my friends and peers when it came college application time. I was confident in expressing myself, and knew what I wanted from a college. When you possess this skill, you are much more likely to write eloquent application essays simply because you know yourself more than the average person.

Summary Assignment for Emotional Intelligence

Watch my video on emotional intelligence on my website Robpasick.com under Self Awareness books links.

Take the online assessment "Do You Lead with Emotional Intelligence" at Harvard Business Review. https://hbr.org/2015/06/quiz-yourself-do-you-lead-with-emotional-intelligence/ (also an appendix in the back of the book)
Do the results surprise you?
Follow their instructions to get feedback from others. Did their feedback surprise you?

Reflect and write up what you learned in your Personal Development Plan (template in appendices). I suggest four paragraphs: one on each aspect of emotional intelligence. You might start with this prompt to start each paragraph: I rate myself _____ on _____...

CHAPTER FOUR

Self-Discovery Step One: Discover Your Strengths

Discover Your Strengths

Everyone has a unique set of strengths and abilities, and the more time you spend using these unique talents, the more successful and satisfied you're likely to be. Dr. Rob often employs several methods to get his students and clients to come to a deeper understanding of their talents.

After using one of these methods, he counsels his students and clients to work with the top five strengths they've identified. It's a comfortable number for goal setting.

One of the easiest methods--**and one Dr. Rob turns to many times**--was developed by Dan Sullivan, founder of StrategicCoach.com. Dan advocates you send e-mails to the people who know you best. Explain that you're going through a self-awareness process and ask them to describe your unique strengths, talents and contributions.

The responses people get are fairly consistent. It shouldn't be too surprising because, for most of us, certain threads weave through our lives. Back in grade school, if you were always organizing neighborhood games or teams, chances are you're still doing it in some fashion in high school and will continue to do it in the years to come.

A similar exercise was developed by Dr. Rob's colleagues at the Center for Positive Organizations at the University of Michigan's Ross School of Business. As with Sullivan's approach, you request positive feedback from people who know you. Then you use this information to create a portrait of your "best self." You can find out more and purchase the Reflected Best Self exercise online.

Another great tool is the Internet-based StrengthsFinder Profile, created by Donald O. Clifton, Tom Rath and a team of scientists from the Gallup Organization. It was later renamed the Clifton StrengthsFinder, and a new web site and book, *Now Discover Your Strengths*, were published in 2007. When you buy the book or purchase the assessment on the website, you get an access code so you can take the assessment online. The program analyzes your answers and comes up with the five most powerful signature themes you display. Based on that, you receive action plans and other activities designed to help you understand how best to use your strengths. Here's where to find out more: StrengthsFinder 2.0 online.

Chapter 4

Your Assignment

> Either do the Sullivan exercise or use the Reflected Best Self template. Send the messages to important people in your life (coaches, mentors, friends, people with whom you've worked or played) and get their feedback on your strengths.
>
> Purchase the StrengthsFinder 2.0 book and assessment test from the Gallup organization. Then take the test.
>
> Then, fill in the "Strengths" Row in your Personal Development Plan (template available online) with your top five strengths.

Thoughts From Lauryn:

After taking the StrengthsFinder test, I was not too surprised by my results. My five main strengths were the Strategic, Woo, Leader, Ideation, and Communication. I asked a few of my friends and family members their opinions on my attributes, and they weren't surprised either. I think that if you are practicing emotional intelligence and self-awareness, your results are likely to validate what you already know about yourself.

Being internally aware of your strengths is important, but this test externalized them for me. I think that when thinking of applying to colleges, high schoolers always focus on negative attributes that won't get them in, not the positive ones. Focusing on strengths, rather than weaknesses, will help you feel more positive going into the application process, but will also help you highlight those strengths in the essay portion of applications.

Identify Your Special Gift

Ask yourself:
- What is my **special gift**?
- Am I using my gift to my **fullest capacity**?
- What do I need to **do today**, to ensure I have the opportunity to use my gift fully in the future?

Dr. Rob was inspired to consider these questions upon hearing a presentation by University of Michigan Ross Business School Professors Bob Quinn and Gretchen Spreitzer at one of his networking events). He learned that the greatest teachers are those who have the greatest capacity for empathy and are able to recognize and nurture the gifts in their students.

Your Reflections

Reflect and then write a hearty full page about your special gift, including examples from the past and consideration on how to best utilize your gift every day. If you feel you have more than one gift, feel free to do this exercise for each gift you identify.
- Going back to childhood, what have I always been good at?
- What do I do that comes easily for me but it is difficult for others?
- I feel energy and joy when I spend my time doing ____.
- If I could overcome the obstacles in my way, I would love to spend my time ____.

Consider what is the special gift of the important people in your life.

Imagine what you can do to nurture and grow your special gift and the gifts of the important people in your life.
- Fill in the blanks: My special gift is ____ and I can use it daily by ____.
- In my experience, reflecting on these questions brings clarity.

Your Assignment

> Summarize your thoughts on your gift in your Personal Development Plan.

Recognize Your Blind Spots

Research shows that often it's not what we see but what we fail to see that causes us to self-destruct. So, it's really important to become aware of our blind spots.

To drive a car safely, we learn to watch the car's blind spots. Essentially, the blind spot in a car is a place behind and to the side of a car that the side- and rear-view mirrors don't show well. In Driver's Ed, we were taught to turn our heads and check the blind spot before changing lanes. Some cars today have blind spot sensors that alert the driver when there's something there if he uses his turn signal.

You have blind spots just like cars on the road. A blind spot is something others see in us that we do not see in ourselves.

Sometimes our strengths and personality traits come paired with vulnerabilities. Someone who is very empathetic might pay more attention to others than she does to herself, leaving her drained and unable to care for others the way she intends. Or, a very organized person may see the world in too strict a manner to put together ideas from disparate settings. Introverted folks may choose to go it alone in times of stress, yet asking for help could solve their issue more quickly and with less suffering.

Chapter 4

Your Reflections

- **You can't know your own blind spots**. Ask others! Poll people who have known you for a long time and ask them to help you identify your blind spots.
- **Be aware of the self-defeating patterns** that can be triggered by blind spots. Teach yourself to let go.
- Once you are aware of your blind spots, **keep them in mind as you make decisions** and interact with others. Ask: Is there any aspect of this where I am giving in to a blind spot?
- Recognize that **you will never please everyone all of the time**. Don't spend hours worrying about what never will be.
- Give yourself **permission to be imperfect**.

Thoughts From Lauryn:
    Asking someone your blind spots can be kind of scary. No one likes criticism, but it's necessary in order to achieve a well-rounded view of yourself. I chose to ask my mom what she thinks my blind spot is. To be honest, I wasn't surprised by the result. I'm a pretty controlling person when I get frustrated, and I know that I need to work on that aspect of my personality.
    Knowing your blind spots is important for the transition to college because it will help you avoid them. Like with the strengths, asking other people is extremely beneficial.

Your Assignment

> Add information on your blind spots to your Personal Development Plan.

Do You Really Know What You Do Best?

    Participating in athletics or other clubs teaches you a lot about yourself. You do a lot of self-assessment, but you learn the most by someone else's assessment of your ability, such as a coach or advisor. Recently Lauryn was preparing for an annual figure skating performance. This performance is a big deal in the town where Lauryn figure skates. It is often just referred to as "the ice show". Being a senior, Lauryn would have a spotlight performance, called "senior salute", in addition to her other show numbers. Below, Lauryn describes what she learned recently while working with her figure skating coach on her senior salute program.

I have been figure skating since I was six years old. I have always loved being on the ice, and have never felt nervous while performing. I really wanted to have a dynamic program that would "wow" the crowd during my senior salute performance at the ice show this year. My idea of wowing the crowd was to do big jumps and fast spins. My coach however, told me that I have always been an elegant skater. She said that I look most natural in my skating performance when I add artistic and graceful elements to my program. She pointed out that I am more likely to look at the crowd and smile when I am "flowing" in my movements on the ice.

I thought about what she had told me about my skating style, and thought back to when I felt most successful in my performances and received the most compliments from the crowd. It was when I was doing more artistic, dance style skating versus the high-level jumps and spins. When I told my parents about my coach's assessment, they were not surprised. They have always received compliments about my graceful skating. They said people really love watching my style of skating because I look so happy and elegant on the ice.

We all have difficulty identifying aspects about ourselves that other people can see clearly. People are notoriously bad at self-reporting. The reasons are complex, including:
- poor self-esteem
- our capacity for self-delusion
- our tendency to be our own worst enemy
- living in a society where it is much easier to give negative feedback rather than positive.

We invite you to take this opportunity to ask others for feedback on what it is that you do well.

Here are some ideas on how you could go about doing this:
- Take time with friends and family who know you best and ask them what they see as your best qualities and strengths. You might explain that you are doing this as part of a class or coaching assignment.
- Be prepared for some surprising answers. Since we are not that good at self-reflection, you may find that how people describe you is very different than what you expect.

Most of us are familiar with Shakespeare's quote "to thine own self be true." **To really know "thine own self," we must have the courage to ask others what they think of us**.

CHAPTER FIVE

Self-Discovery Step Two: Define Your Interests and Passions

Thoughts From Lauryn:
Before diving into this chapter, I viewed my interests as things that simply made me happy. Don't get me wrong, your interests SHOULD make you happy, but they should also serve as assets that you can utilize throughout the application process.
Yes, it's easy to spend hours a day stressing over the application process, but you shouldn't let that take away from your interests and passions. By maintaining passions and interests while completing the application process, your essays will most likely represent a clearer picture of who you are.

Discovering Your Passion

"Though, consumed with the hot fire of his purpose, Ahab in all his thoughts and actions ever had in view the ultimate capture of Moby Dick; though he seemed ready to sacrifice all mortal interests to that one passion..."
-Herman Melville, Moby Dick (1851)

A key to becoming a more self-aware is to identify what you are passionate about. The problem is that this search often is a lifetime pursuit. Many people have difficulty identifying their passion. Some find it later in life.

To discover your passion, begin by identifying your main interests. By knowing what your interests are, you are able to focus your activities, utilize your talents, and make choices which take you closer and closer to discovering your passions.

Most of you already have already made important choices in your life. For instance, if you are interested in a certain sport you know that, in general, your interests draw you to activities related to that sport.

Your Reflections

Here are some key questions which will enable you to identify your interests and your passions:

What do you stand for?

- What do you **care about deeply**?
- Is there a societal problem for which you would like to **contribute a solution**?
- I always tell myself that anything worth achieving requires **facing distinct difficulties, experiencing internal struggle, and facing big risk**.
  1. For what goal, are you willing to **risk everything**?
  2. For what are you willing to **sacrifice or even suffer to achieve**?

What excites you?

Identify your peak moments in life so far. Think of the times when you felt your best, when you felt excited and proud, and when you most felt that time slipped away quickly. When you think of these moments, you are probably recalling moments when your passion was most intense. By discovering what you were doing at those moments, you reveal your passions.

- What did you **love to do as a child**?
- When you have had **a great day**, what was it you were doing and what are you not doing?
- Passion is about emotion. What topic most **evokes a strong emotional reaction** in you?
- What do you love to do with **your free time**?
- What activities **give you energy and joy**?
- If you **had $1 million**, what would you do?

Create a "**passion masterpiece**" such as a scrapbook or poster. To further discover your passion, begin to clip articles, photos, song lyrics, and images that ignite your spirit. Create a collage full of pictures that excite you. As you begin to build upon your collection, notice to what you are drawn and to what you are indifferent. Add your passion masterpiece (or an image of it or a link to it) to your Personal Development Plan.

Bonus Activity - Ask other people what they think you are passionate about. You might consider talking in person, video chatting, or sending an email to at least three people who know you well to ask them what they see you most passionate about.

Passion Summary Assignment

Unlike for Strengths and Personality, I have found no useful online "passion test" to assign. The way to uncover your passions is to reflect and get feedback from others.

This section contains reflection questions. Now, write a short summary of your passions and interests in your Personal Development Plan.

CHAPTER SIX

Self-Discovery Step Three: Understand Your Personality

Discover Your Personality

Personality is a characteristic that has been studied extensively by psychologists over the last several decades. Research has defined five aspects of personality. These "big five" are:
- **O**penness to Experience - do you prefer change to the status quo?
- **C**onscientiousness (work ethic) - are you organized and disciplined?
- **E**xtraversion - do you enjoy meeting and interacting with new people? Do you recharge yourself socially or alone?
- **A**greeableness - are you accommodating or firm?
- **N**atural Reactions - are you relaxed and calm or excitable/anxious?

These big five personality spectra are often described by their acronym, **OCEAN**.

Your Reflection
For each of these, where do you feel you are on a range of high/middle/low?

The Michigan Model of Leadership

Some call it "personality types." Some call it "mindset." Some measure it with the Myers-Briggs. Others with the DISC. No matter what you call it, or how you measure it, these personality differences do matter.

Why are they so popular? Because they make such intuitive sense. They are important tools in our attempt to gain better self-awareness, leverage our emotional intelligence, and improve our performance as human beings.

Dr. Rob uses a model developed by Robert Quinn, Kim Cameron, and Jeff DeGraff at the University of Michigan Ross School of Business. It is called the "Competing Values Framework" and is now the "Michigan Leadership Model". He likes it because it is direct, intuitive, and based on solid research. It also has colors associated with it.

Here is how we describe the four basic personality differences:

1. "**Collaborators**" are people who care about relationships, care about people's feelings, like to mentor, and develop other people. First and foremost, their mindset is to look at relationships and how their actions affect others and how they are affected by other people's actions. Like the sun nurturing all living things, we call these folks "yellow".

2. "**Competitors**" are the people who tend to focus on producing results, setting goals, and achieving these goals. Like the IBM salesforce, we call this type "blues".

3. "**Creatives**" are people who like to generate new ideas, innovate, embrace change and constantly search for new solutions to old problems. Constantly introducing new ideas for growth, we refer to this type as the "greens".

4. "**Controls**" care deeply about rules and processes. They focus on ways to get the job done most efficiently. In honor of the barristers in London who bound their law books in red tape, we call these people the "reds".

There is one more very important point to remember well. Most of us human beings are not totally one color. Generally, most people as a blend. Most of us have strong elements of two of the characteristics; we can function adequately in a third type, but rarely do we see people who excel and feel strong about their capability in all four types.

Using Dr. Rob as an example, he describes himself as having a ton of yellow, lots of green, a little blue, and very little red. If were to describe himself by distributing 100 points, he would be:

35 Yellow,

30 Green,

25 Blue,

10 Red.

So here is your challenge. Take the 100 point test. If you had to describe your personality, using the four colors of the "Competing Values Framework" model, how would you distribute the points?

Yellow?

Green?

Blue?

Red?

Now, what have you learned about yourself from this exercise?

Through other relatively quick assessments, it is possible to understand your personality even better. However, is it important to recognize that these assessments depend on information which comes directly from the individual taking the assessment.

Since human beings are notoriously poor at understanding themselves, these personalities have a severe limitation. They are describing the individual solely based on input from the individual.

In this section, you will take one of these online assessments. Yet, it is also important to include feedback from others.

Your Assignment

Follow this link to a website where you will be asked to answer 120 questions. You will then receive the PDF of the results of the survey which will enable you to better understand your personality. Here is the link. 123test.com/big-five-personality-theory/

Please fill in your OCEAN test results on your Personal Development Plan.

CHAPTER SEVEN
Self-Discovery Step Four: Manage your Energy and Your Body

Thoughts From Lauryn:
Before studying mindfulness, I hadn't put much thought into how self-awareness can relate to your body. Like I mentioned earlier in the book, I took a mindfulness class my Junior year. In that class, I learned that being mindful about your body is deliberate. You can be extremely healthy physically and just the opposite mentally. Really, you can make anything a mindful activity if you have the right mentality.

I've always ran to de-stress. Running is a repetitive motion, so I find it very easy to think and evaluate the stressors in my life. I think that one important thing to note from this chapter is that managing your body is not necessarily exercise, which is what I think most people default to (at least I did!) Managing your body can simply be writing down your feelings or thoughts from the day.

Tips from a 96-Year-Old on Staying Fit in Mind, Body, and Spirit

Rob's mother-in-law, Jean Carino, at age 96 continues to be strong in mind, body, and spirit. The key to her being able to sustain health and vitality at 96 is that she pays attention to all three of these areas. Her interests include reading, games such as Mah-jongg, and golf. She is an active member of her church. Inspired by her, Dr. Rob has developed these four tips on how to stay strong in mind, body, and spirit throughout your life.

Four Tips on how to Stay Strong in Mind, Body, and Spirit

1. Take an honest inventory
2. Make regular habits and rituals to stay fit
3. Be mindful in all that you do
4. Practice love.

First, on a regular basis, take an honest inventory and give yourself a grade on how well you are doing in taking care of yourself on:

- Mind (0-10 scale, 10 excellent)
- Body (0-10 scale, 10 excellent)
- Spirit (0-10 scale, 10 excellent)

Second, create regular habits or rituals to be sure to do something daily to stay fit in all three areas. Some examples are:
- Journal--writing and/or drawing
- Meditate, pray
- Spend time outdoors, enjoy nature
- Engage in a creative activity
- Exercise
- Participate in sports
- Play, including games with friends and family
- Engage in stimulating conversations
- Read meaningful literature

Third, be mindful in all that you do.
- Do one thing at a time
- Be aware of the impact you have on others
- Do good for others without seeking benefit for yourself

Fourth, practice love.
- Look for specific ways to love yourself
- Love your family and friends, this may take some creativity when they are far away from you.
- Love the world you live in and protect the earth

Your Assignment

> Imagine you are 22, and you are looking back on your secret sauce for having had a successful college experience. What ingredients would have gone into your secret sauce for health in mind, body, and spirit? Describe them in a letter to yourself. Date the letter and revisit it over the years.

Body and Body Image

For most young people body and body image are primary concerns and are often the source deep anxiety. A major part of self-awareness is to develop an accurate sense of how you feel about your body.

Chapter 7

Your Reflections

- List the positive qualities that make your body unique to you.
- What do you do each day/week/month to care for your physical body?
- How do others support you and how do you engage with others to eat and drink healthfully?
- How do others support you in health?
- How do you engage with others to participate in healthy activities?
- What positive changes could you make in the next week/month toward better self-care?
- What resources are available to you if you or a friend are having thoughts or actions of an unhealthy lifestyle?
- Who would be supportive of you in making changes toward a more positive self-image?

Your Assignment

Write a paragraph summarizing what you do well to care for your body. Write a second paragraph outlining any plans you have to improve your self-care.

CHAPTER EIGHT

Self-Discovery Step Five: Care for Your Mind

Is Your Thinking Making You Miserable?

When you begin thinking about or apply to colleges you may become anxious. You be glad to know that many people experience anxiety in times of the unknown. Usually it is not a specific situation that makes a person anxious but it's how the person interprets the situation. You may also be forcing yourself to be cautious or pessimistic about certain colleges because you think it will make it easier to take if you get rejected from that college.

You can learn to change your thinking to cope with the anxiety. As a psychologist, Dr. Rob practices a therapy known as Cognitive Behavioral Therapy, which teaches people to recognize faulty irrational thinking, and to replace it with a more rational, cognitively based approach to life. It has been the cornerstone of Dr. Rob's personal and professional approach.

Here are some of the core concepts of Cognitive Behavioral Therapy that you can use in your daily life:

- Recognize when you are making yourself upset by clinging to irrational and faulty thinking.
- Strive to understand HOW others are thinking about situations before you judge them.
- When you are troubled, get past any stigma that you have that therapy is a sign of weakness. Rather, reinterpret your thinking to see therapy as a sign of strength and courage.
- Recognize that there are three musts that hold us back: I must do well, you must treat me well, the world must be easy and fair.
- Stop 'shoulding' on yourself (e.g. telling yourself you *should* be loved and approved of by everyone for everything you do).

Today there are online approaches to help people manage their anxiety and depression. If you feel you cannot manage your anxiety and stress, seek help from any of the trusted resources we listed in chapter one.

Chapter 8

Challenge Your Irrational Ideas

Many of life's problems stem not so much from the things that happen to us as from how we interpret these events. Whether we realize it or not, most of us carry around one or more irrational ideas that act as filters for our experiences. These may cause us to react more strongly and inappropriately to events than is warranted.

In his research, psychologist Albert Ellis identified a famous "dirty dozen" of these irrational ideas. See if you recognize yourself in any of them:

1. People **must be loved** by significant others for almost everything they do.
2. Certain acts are **awful or wicked**, and the people who perform them should **be damned**.
3. It's **horrible** when things are not the way we like them to be.
4. Human misery is invariably externally caused and **forced on us** by outside people and events.
5. If something is or may be dangerous or fearsome, we **should be terribly upset** and obsess about it endlessly.
6. It's **easier to avoid** than to face life's difficulties and responsibilities.
7. We **absolutely need** something or someone stronger or greater than ourselves **on which to rely**.
8. We **should be thoroughly competent**, intelligent and achieving in all possible respects.
9. Because something once strongly affected our life, it **should indefinitely** affect it.
10. We must have certain and **perfect control over things**.
11. Human happiness can be achieved by inertia and **inaction**.
12. We have **virtually no control over our emotions** and cannot help feeling disturbed about things.

Once you learn to recognize your irrational baggage, you can challenge those assumptions as they arise--and close the lid on them.

Your Assignment

Which of the twelve irrational ideas do you recognize? Circle your top three that are most pertinent to you. Reflect on ways in which these three might interfere with your health and success. Develop a plan for learning to challenge these thoughts.

Add your top three irrational beliefs to the Personal Development Plan. Describe your plan to counteract these beliefs.

Chapter 8

Thoughts From Ali:
I know first-hand how difficult it may be to open up to your parents about a problem that has recently been irritating you. Sometimes, it may be easier to talk about such a problem with a friend. Talk to a friend that you know has your back and is willing to help. It's important that you know there are always resources available to help with whatever it is you might be going through. Also, keep a watchful eye for any of your friends that seem to be struggling emotionally.

One month during school, I happened to notice one of my friends stopped attending school after his parents had divorced. I decided to have a one-on-one conversation with him and offer up some advice considering I had gone through the same thing. This friend of mine really appreciated the outreach and support. It took just one small gesture from me, that meant the world to this friend of mine.

Get the Help You Need

We often don't hesitate to seek expert advice when we're trying to learn a skill like golf or cooking. Sometimes we seek out other experts--therapists or coaches--when something feels broken. But sometimes when we are having extreme difficulty, we don't seek help at all because we are fearful or have feelings of shame. Help is available, and no one should have to go it alone.

Take a look at yourself, and make sure you ask for the help you need.
- If you think you have a psychiatric problem, talk to someone you closely trust (preferably an adult)
  - ❏ Parents/ Guardians
  - ❏ School Counselor
  - ❏ Trusted Teacher
- If you have a health problem, go to a doctor.
- If there's trouble on the home front, talk to your family about seeing a therapist.
- If you're having a spiritual crisis, seek out a clergy person.
- If you're not sure what you should do, consult a friend or someone close to you.
- Pray for guidance or meditate for clarity

Your Assignment

> Consider what you need and why you hold back from giving to yourself. Usually it is something like fear of finding out something you don't want to know or cost in addressing a problem. If there is something that's holding you back, it won't go away on its own, so it is important to make a plan for addressing it. Whom will you ask for help? By when? How will you do it?

How to Start Meditating

For a variety of reasons, Dr. Rob suggests learning to meditate and develop a practice of mindfulness. Through meditation, one learns to focus attention, control negative thoughts, and achieve peacefulness.

Often, people are overwhelmed with how difficult they believe meditation can be. As a way to get started, here is simple method from the book "How to Meditate" by Eknath Easwaran. By devoting just thirty minutes a day, they learn how to successfully maintain a meditation and mindfulness practice.

Thirty minutes a day is a lot in the beginning. You can build up to it with a smaller time commitment.

Five steps to get started meditating

1. Find a passage of literature which you find inspirational. This could be a poem, a prayer, a song lyric, etc. Spend 10 minutes reading the passage.
2. Memorize a portion of this passage
3. With your passage in mind, sit in a calm space with your eyes closed for 10 minutes.
4. While focusing on your breathing, on each exhale breath repeat one word of your passage. For example: If your passage is the "Serenity Prayer", with your first breath you would say "God," followed by the second breath, "grant", the third "me" ...etc., and continue until you have completed the passage. If you lose your concentration or place, start over from beginning of the sentence you were on.
5. After your 10 minutes of meditation, write reflectively in a journal for another 10 minutes. The only rule is to write something, whether it is a few words or several pages.

An Alternative

You can use a meditation timer app on your phone to guide and support your practice. Once you commit to meditating for a certain time, you can set the app to play a gentle sound at the end of the time. The app can also log your meditation (date, time, duration).

Chapter 8

Sophisticated apps can remind you to meditate, turn off the sound and notifications on your device when you meditate, play soothing sounds to help you drown out nearby distractions, give you access to recorded guided meditation audio files, and connect you with others who meditate at the same time. Insight(free, available for iPhone and Android phones) is a great app to explore.

Give it a Try!

Since many people are working at a rapid pace and multitasking much of the time, we recommend this practice as a way to slow down and regain control of their mind.

Thoughts From Lauryn:
I find apps helpful to guide meditations. Sometimes, it can be difficult or awkward to meditate on your own. Using an app can guide you through the motions of meditation. One of my favorites is the calm app, which is free to download. Often, many smartwatches have meditation apps built in to them, making it easy to meditate anywhere.

Practice Self-Reflection

Meditation is only one of the ways to practice self-reflection. You may prefer to do it in connection with your faith. You may want to keep a journal. Or you may prefer talking with someone on a regular basis--your significant other, a friend or even another couple. Sometimes it's easier to be open and reflective with those who aren't part of your immediate family.

Your Reflections

- Set aside time for reflection.
- Find an activity--meditation, yoga, writing, prayer, conversation--that allows you to express your inner life.
- Keep a journal.
- Find an aid, perhaps a book or an online site, to help you and give you encouragement.
- Turn to a 12-step program if you need help with an addiction.
- Take advantage of faith-based spiritual retreats and study groups.
- Talk to a therapist if you need special help.
- Take a class to learn ways to stimulate self-reflection.
- Use your drive time for reflection.

Dr. Rob's Delayed Grief over Grandpa Izzie

Chapter 8

    Grief is an emotional reaction to loss. It is what we feel when we lose someone, something, or even a goal. Grief is the process we go through in the aftermath of that loss. Our problem is that our grief is often short-circuited. We have not been allowed, or do not allow ourselves, adequate time to grieve over our losses. Beginning with boyhood and continuing throughout the life cycle, we are told that the appropriate way to handle loss of any kind is to acknowledge it stoically then to get on with life, quickly, which usually means acting like the loss never occurred.

    This simply does not work. If a loss is not adequately mourned, it can have adverse effects on a person's psychological development, particularly on the way the person behaves in future relationships.

    A few years ago, I became aware of the consequences of not having mourned the loss of my maternal grandfather, who committed suicide in 1970 when I was twenty-three. Here's the story of what reignited the grief so many years later.

    After having put off cleaning the garage for months, I decided to confront the tangled extension cords, the dust-covered garden tools, and the boxes filled with items long forgotten and not missed but somehow too important to be thrown away.

    Reluctantly, I dug in. Not far into the sorting and tossing, I paused to examine the contents of a gray metal box. I was unprepared for my reaction as I discovered an old electric sander with a manila tag on it. I recognized it immediately as a pawn ticket from the shop where my grandfather had worked most of his life. In his beautiful handwriting I could still make out the words, "Henry Washington, June, 1958," the name of the man who had hocked the sander and the date it had to be claimed. Evidently Mr. Washington had not claimed it on time, so my grandfather had bought it cut-rate. Gazing at that ticket, I realized I had not seen anything in my grandfather's handwriting since his death in 1970.

    I remembered myself, as a child, living with my parents and grandparents in a small suburban home, eagerly awaiting the return of Grandpa Izzie from the pawnshop on Saturday night. He would often bring home an array of drills, radios, and other unclaimed items. I always thought of them as his special gifts to me. Holding that ticket, I felt the rush of memories it summoned. It occurred to me that the small piece of cardboard was the only memento I still had of Izzie.

    During the Detroit riots of 1967, the pawnshop was burned down. Less dramatically but just as inevitably, Izzie, out of work for the first time in his life, began deteriorating, too. For income, he rekindled his old habit of gambling; as the losses mounted, his drinking increased. He began issuing suicide threats. I was teaching school in New York City when I received the call from my father. Izzie's final threat was not idle. He had killed himself by swallowing jeweler's acid, just as he had threatened many times before.

    As I showed my wife and kids that tag, I felt myself fighting back the tears. In a way I wished they would finally flow. Due to the mixed feelings associated with his suicide, I had never been able to cry over the loss of my grandfather. The situation was made more complicated by the family's decision to keep the cause of death a secret. At his age, we figured why dishonor his memory? No one would doubt the family story that this heavy smoker had had a heart attack. Little did I understand that keeping the suicide a secret would block me from adequately mourning the grandfather I had loved so dearly. My friends knew my grandfather had died, but out of loyalty to my family I could share with no one my anguish over the manner of his death.

In the years immediately following his death, my feelings about Izzie alternated between guilt and anger. As an only child growing up in a house of adults, my specialty had been to keep everyone cheerful, especially this alternately morose and exuberant man. I had failed to cheer him up this time. It seemed perfectly natural for me to major in psychology in college. As a psych student, moreover, shouldn't I have recognized the warning signs of suicide and been able to prevent it? Maybe if I hadn't left home, he wouldn't have become so depressed. Maybe I should have invited him to visit me in New York City. The list of "shoulds" and maybes was long and persistent whenever I was reminded of Izzie, which happened often since I like to listen to Detroit Tiger baseball on the radio. Izzie always seemed to have a portable radio stuck in his ear, listening to Ernie Harwell, the voice of the Tigers. (Izzie liked to call them the Pussycats in those days of constant fifth-place finishes.)

The only match for my guilt was my anger. Somehow, I could not easily forgive him for having tarnished two of my life's greatest joys. Izzie had always been my number one fan. How often I had heard him say, "Robbie, you're going to be a great man someday." With his encouragement I had made two important decisions in 1970: to apply to graduate school and to ask my girlfriend, Pat, to marry me. How sad and disappointed I felt that he had not waited around to hear about my acceptance at Harvard and to attend our wedding. If he had really cared about me, he would not have taken his life just four months before the wedding.

As the years went by, though, sorrow emerged as the dominant emotion. I missed him. I ached at the memory of him waking me up in the morning by imitating an alarm clock or driving me and my friends to high school in his '61 Chevy Nova. "Who's kicking me in the amplifier?" he'd ask the laughing teenagers in the backseat.

I was sad, too, that my own sons never had a chance to meet Izzie. They would have enjoyed this slight, handsome man who made bad jokes, spoke his own foreign tongue especially designed for his grandchildren, and who would pile all the kids in the neighborhood into his small car to take us to an afternoon Tigers game.

As I showed my sons the ticket, I was pleased that they, too, have had wonderful relationships with their own grandfathers. I know, of course, that they were in no way responsible for their grandfathers' well-being. This thought helped me to realize that I wasn't to blame, and Izzie wasn't to be punished for taking his own life. Now I can understand how painful his undiagnosed manic-depression must have been. No, the most painful facet of Izzie's death -- missing him -- was simply a function of his passing away. Suicide and heart attacks have equal status there.

I detached the tag and gently cleaned off the dust. I realized that maybe a pawn ticket may be an appropriate memory for this man. In some ways he had pawned his own life away. But in many ways, I owe a debt to him as well. He contributed much to who I am today: to the development of my playful side; to my courage to take risks; and to my love of baseball. Now I am determined not to allow his manner of death to obliterate the spirit of the man. To me he had been a hero, a dapper guy in a Fedora and a natty sport coat with his shoes always shined. As I placed the ticket in my wallet, I vowed never to stow it or his memory away again.

Your Assignment

> Grief occurs not only over death. Grief can be a reaction to almost any type of loss, and we have all experienced many. I invite you to reflect on your own losses and to ask yourself how adequately you have mourned these losses.

CHAPTER NINE
Self-Discovery Step Six: Invest in Your Relationships

Thoughts From Lauryn:
After my sophomore year of high school, my family moved from Ohio to Michigan. I found that this move made me feel somewhat disconnected from my friends in Ohio, even though we talked every day.

When I travel back to Ohio, I make a conscious effort to see my friends in one way or another. Investing in relationships is not only beneficial for simply maintaining them, but for forming future connections as well.

The Harvard Study of Adult Development

The Harvard Study of Adult Development may be the longest study of adult life that's ever been done. For 75 years, they've tracked the lives of 724 men, year after year, asking about their work, their home lives, their health, and of course asking all along the way without knowing how their life stories were going to turn out. The clearest message that we get from this 75-year study is this: **Good relationships keep us happier and healthier.** Period.

Throughout Dr. Rob's 40-year career as a psychologist, **he believes most strongly that the cornerstone of good relationships is self-awareness.**

Here's the link to a TED talk on the Harvard Study of Adult Development. https://www.ted.com/talks/robert_waldinger_what_makes_a_good_life_lessons_from_the_longest_study_on_happiness

Your Reflection

What is your major takeaway from the TED talk?

When Oprah Calls Dr. Rob
Thoughts from Dr. Rob:
When my kids were teenagers in the early 1990s, I got really caught up in writing books about men. I'd published two books, *Men in Therapy* and *Awakening from the Deep Sleep,* about men and their relationships and how they should live their lives differently. As the books were very well received, I quickly followed with another book, *What Every Man Needs to Know.*

As I began to experience a fair degree of success, I started to act as though my time as an author and thought leader was more important than my time as a father and husband. I became obsessed with traveling, giving workshops, and contemplating what my next book was going to be.

One spring, we scheduled a long-overdue family vacation on Hilton Head Island. My cousins from Texas joined us, too. Only three days into the week-long trip, my assistant in Ann Arbor called to say, "You got a call from a producer on the Oprah show. They have an opening on the show and they want you to be on it." But the opening was just two days away--in the middle of our vacation.

Without hesitating or consulting my family, I made arrangements to fly to Chicago. Later, I told my wife and kids how excited I was. They were gracious about my leaving, even helping me buy a new suit to wear on the show, but I didn't think about the fact that I was leaving them and my cousins.

It wasn't until I returned a few days later to a rather icy reception that it dawned on me: I had been so caught up in my success that I had put my own need for fame ahead of the family's need for togetherness and time with Dad.

I'd done a lot of things in my life, but the fact that I was on The Oprah Winfrey Show was special. Later, my friends started calling me "Oprah Man" and asking me what Oprah was like. I'm not ashamed to admit that it went straight to my head. I had become seduced by success. It was amazing how easy it was for me to set aside some of my basic values. And the irony of it, of course, was that my book was about how men should shed their self-centered behavior. I found myself becoming a case study for my own book!

It took a while, but eventually I came to my senses. Being a good dad and good husband were more important than being on Oprah. It was time for me to back off and reset my priorities.

Cultivate Friendships

Reconnecting with old friends and making and maintaining new ones is essential to our growth and development. Friends are vital to health and happiness; they can even help reduce stress.

Studies have shown that people who have intimate relationships are more likely to survive heart attacks and less likely to develop cancer and serious infections. There also is a strong correlation between a lack of social relationships and high blood pressure, smoking and obesity.

Without close friends, we battle loneliness and feel disconnected from the past. We often pine for the sense of connectedness we had as kids. Lots of things get in the way of maintaining friendships, including the competitive nature of our society. But we should try diligently to resist these pressures.

Thoughts From Ali:

As a senior in high school, I cannot stress enough how important it is to be active in your community. Participate in at least one of the following:

club sports, school sports, theatre, volunteer organizations, or school clubs. As I take a look at my friend group, I realize that almost all of them stem from an extracurricular activity we've participated in together. These are the same friends who I know will have my back and ensure I won't feel lonely or disconnected.

Your Reflections

- Cultivate your relationship with your parents, because these ties are the prototypes for your relationships with peers.
- Stay connected with friends; make time for personal interactions while not getting overwhelmed with social media
- Look for ways to open up to current friends: Plan a trip or outing. Talk about something you usually might not be inclined to bring up.
- Identify the obstacles that tend to get in the way of your friendships: fear of rejection, unresolved conflicts, insufficient time, competitiveness, past failures.
- Recognize that friendships aren't just about "being liked"; they're also about taking care of yourself by feeling connected to others.
- Call at least one friend a week.
- Do something--join a group, take a class, learn a new hobby or become a volunteer--that will put you in contact with others.
- Don't create a situation where all of your friendships are tied to work or groups you belong to.
- Be open and honest about yourself.
- Make couple friendships and set up times to spend with couples you and your mate both like

Your Assignment

> Make a list of your friends. Identify how you became friends and what keeps you interested in the friendship. How much effort do you put into the friendship? How hard are you willing to work to make new friendships in college?

Forget Trying to Control People

Leaders worry themselves to death over how to get people to do what they want them to do. Dr. Rob's book, *Conversations with My Old Dog,* is a series of poems about the

"talks" he used to have with his aging yellow lab Lucy. The poem "Control" includes these lines:
> *We people spend much of our time on the illusion of control--*
> *we order our lives and try*
> *to order the lives of others.*
> *However, we learn--as with our dogs--*
> *that we may get folks to sit*
> *but never to stay.*

Rob offers the same advice to the people he coaches. **It's difficult enough to control your own behavior; it's a losing proposition to try to control others'**. Learn to appreciate their behavior instead.

Our Reflections

- No matter what your title, **treat everyone with respect**.
- Take the time to **engage people**; ask questions and let them ask you questions. Give honest answers. Listen to their responses. It's better when you can hear from others what they think should be done. Collectively, you can try to control the outcomes.
- Be willing to **accept the mood and behavior swings of others**. They, like you, are human.
- Don't overestimate how well you know even the people closest to you--your siblings, your friends, your parents. **No matter how familiar you are with them, you cannot control them**. Learn to enjoy the surprises rather than treating them as a sign of irrationality or rebellion.
- Keep in mind that **groups are even more complex than individuals**. Appreciate the good things that can emerge when everyone feels empowered to speak.
- **Give yourself a pat on the back** or make a note of the times when you manage to treat the behavior of others in a more positive way than you once would have.
- **Work at controlling the things you can control**: eat healthfully, exercise regularly and seek sources of inspiration to boost your emotional well-being.
- At best, **you can only control one person: yourself**.

Your Assignment

Consider - are you someone who tries to control people? If so, is this something you want to change about yourself? Write out your plan for change.

Consider - are you someone who is afraid to stand up for yourself? If so, is this something you want to change about yourself? Write out your plan for change.

Chapter 9

> In your plan for change, describe why you need to change, what you plan to change, by when, from whom you need support, and how you will do it.

The Importance of Making Connections

Here are my 10 key do's and don'ts for being successfully connected to others:

1. **DO** help those with whom you are connected.
2. **DO NOT** expect reciprocity on a one to one basis. Help others without expecting that they will help you in return.
3. **DO** build your network by joining and actively participating in community and workplace groups. The key word here is ACTIVELY.
4. **DO NOT** just show up. To be well connected you have to volunteer, do some work, and give back to the organization.
5. **DO** seek to be connected to a diverse group of individuals from different spheres of society and different types of work.
6. **DO NOT** hang out and only connect with people who are only like yourself.
7. **DO** actively relate to others when you go to events. The best way to relate is to show interest in the other person by asking meaningful questions. If you are shy or introverted, make a plan ahead of time with conversation starters and a few details to share about yourself.
8. **DO NOT** only talk about yourself. An elevator speech is fine, but it is more powerful to show interest in the other people at the event.
9. **DO** keep in touch with your friends, family, and colleagues on a regular basis.
10. **DO NOT** rely on email to stay connected. Set up times for coffee, drinks, or lunch, hang out at places where you are likely to run into your network, and pick up the phone.

Remember, at every level of life, the living world works through cooperation. We are all interconnected and interdependent.

Checklist to Grow Connections

- Ask like-minded individuals to **get together** for coffee, lunch, or a drink *(at least weekly)*.
- Go to **networking** meetings
- Hang out in a public place such as the coffee shop where you are **likely to run into people** with whom you could share ideas (and of course strike up conversations with these people).
- **Post your ideas** or links to good articles on social media *(at least weekly)*.
- **Send interesting articles** to people who might also find them interesting.

- **Respond** with more than "I like" to other people's posts *(daily or several times a week)*. For example, you can respond with a question.

Your Assignment

> Do an honest assessment of how well you are able to network (on a scale of 0-10 with 10 being excellent).
> Consider what you do well and what you want to do better.
> Create a plan for improving your networking skills. In your plan, detail why you need to improve, what you will improve, how you will do this, by when, and from whom you need support.

Fill those Buckets

Authors Tom Rath and Donald O. Clifton used research by the Gallup Organization to craft the bestseller *How Full Is Your Bucket?*

Their basic theory is that we start out every day with a bucket that is emptied or filled by what others say and do to us. We each also have a dipper. We can use it to fill other people's buckets by delivering positive messages or we can dip from others' buckets by delivering negative messages. When we fill others' buckets, we replenish our own. And when we take from others' buckets, we deplete our own.

The process is contagious. If you fill others' buckets with positive messages, they will carry it forward. So, if you work for me and I build you up, you're more likely to build up the people you come in contact with. If I drain your bucket, you're more likely to dump on others.

David loved playing sports. Although he was not the best on any given team, he had adequate athletic skills, and he played with passion. David also encouraged others to be passionate about the sport.

When David entered high school, he found that it was very competitive to be noticed by the coaches of the high school football team and to get playing time. David attended all practices, mandatory and optional. He asked the coaches for advice on getting better at his position, and he paid attention to the game if he was on the sidelines.

Not only did David focus on improving his football skills he encouraged his teammates to work hard and have fun. He was always the first to congratulate a teammate on a job well done, or to encourage one who was disappointed in himself during the game.

By the end of the season, David was a starter on the freshman football team, and he was often called on by coaches to fill other positions during critical plays. He was also well liked by all of his teammates. At the football end of the season awards banquet, David was given the "Leadership Award".

David did not work hard and encourage others for shallow reasons such as awards and glory, but because he genuinely had a good attitude. You know what they say about attitudes: "***Attitudes are contagious. Is yours worth catching?***"

Your Reflections

- **Keep track of the abundances of your day--**the times when someone has been nice to you or when you've done someone a favor, when a meeting has gone particularly well or when you've offered someone praise or encouragement. Jot them down on paper or on your device. People remember and respect those who make them feel special. You really have only three choices when you respond to others: praise, ignore or criticize.
- **Turn a negative into a positive**. If you notice someone seems out of sorts or is struggling, ask what's wrong. Find out what kind of help they need or whether they have the resources to get the job done.
- **Be genuine about your praise**. Don't manufacture it for the sake of appearances.
- Keep in mind research by psychologist John Gottman that **shows healthy relationships have a ratio of five positive interactions for every negative one**. So if you're handing out more corrections than pats on the back, people are going to start feeling bad about themselves.
- **Be specific about what you praise**. Highlight a report the person submitted or a comment they made in a meeting.
- **Keep track of your own daily achievements**, however small.
- Remember: **Nine out of 10 people say they're more productive when they're around positive people**.
- **Fill another's bucket and you automatically fill your own.**
- **Smile**. Nothing gives as much happiness as the gift of awareness.

Your Assignment

Read the student quote below. For the next week, keep track of how well you fill the buckets of those around you. No matter how good you are at being positive with other people, there's almost always room for improvement.

> "One activity that stayed with me was when we went around the room and had to compliment each other. It is such a simple task in principle but was actually rather difficult to think of compliments on the spot for people that I had only known for a few weeks. I find that it is easy to notice when someone does something wrong, and it is easy to tell that person that they messed up. However, unless I am on the lookout for

> the things I like about others, many positives go unnoticed and upraised. Since that activity I have tried to more actively look for the positives of people around me, and when I see them, to let those people know. Everyone likes a sincere compliment so why shouldn't we give them out more?"

Apologize When You're Wrong

- **Love does not mean never having to say you're sorry** or wrong about something.
- **Leaders aren't more perfect than other people**. Be strong enough to admit a mistake and set the record straight.
- **Don't try to hide your areas of vulnerability**. Everyone has them.
- **Recognize when you are being domineering**.
- **Talk it out** with someone you have been upset with--the sooner, the better.
- **Learn to apologize without adding blame**. An example of what not to say is "I apologize ... but you provoked me.
- **Avoid creating a triangle** by bringing other people into the conflict. You may seek advice but be aware of the difference between that and gossiping or getting your side of the story out first. It comes down to this: "**Are you seeking help or are you trying to change someone's opinion of the person you have a conflict with?**"

Your Assignment

> Keep track for a week of how often you apologize, and whether you are successful at apologizing without blaming the other person.

Learn People's Stories

Oral historian Alan Lomax once said, "The essence of America is not within the headline heroes ... but in the everyday folks who live and die unknown, yet leave their dreams as legacies."

We all have a desire to connect as human beings, and everyone has a story. If you take the time to discover these stories, you will forge strong bonds. Ask simple questions-- "Where'd you grow up?" "How many people are in your family?" Pay attention to little things.

A very high achieving college athlete seemed to have everything going for him. He was a top athlete at a highly rated university, and was doing well academically. He had many options for his future, and he appeared happy and well adjusted.

However, his past story was different than the successful student he portrayed on a daily basis. He grew up in poverty, and he not only had to overcome those struggles but his mother passed away from breast cancer when he was only 16, leaving him to be cared for by his brother who was only 18 at that time. He worked hard to stay in school and excel in sports so that he could get a scholarship to college. He also encouraged his younger brother to follow his example, and that little brother earned a basketball scholarship at a top university.

Most people will never know this student's story. He's not embarrassed to tell it, but people usually don't ask him about his life before being a football star. As a result of his life experiences, he plans to use his athletic and academic success to work with kids to encourage them to overcome adversity and follow their dreams.

Your Reflections

- **Ask people about their lives**--and listen to their answers. "If you take the time to listen, you'll find wisdom, wonder and poetry in their lives," writes David Isay in *Listening Is an Act of Love*.
- **Ask family members about their day.**
- **Ask people about their pictures**.
- People generally love recounting tales from the past. Get them to open up with simple questions about their families and **where they once lived or went to school**.
- **Look around**. Notice what people are wearing. What you see is a jumping off point for a conversation.
- Learn to **ask the kinds of questions that get people talking about themselves**.
- **Tell your own stories**, including those of people who helped you get where you are today.
- Keep in mind these words from Gabriel Garcia Marquez: **"What matters most in life is not what happens to you, but what you remember and how you remember it."**

Your Assignment

Please visit storycorps.org to listen to a few stories, and then interview a trusted family member for comments on the thesis of this book: emotional success is a function of your ability to manage relationships well.

Respond to any or all of the following prompts, or discuss another aspect of this exercise that was meaningful to you.
- Discuss why you choose to interview this person.
- What were your key questions going into the interview?
- Did the interview go as you expected? Explain.

- Write one or two meaningful takeaways from this interview/exercise.
- What piece of insight or advice did you receive that you think is worth passing on to a friend?

Avoid Cutoffs

When people have a relationship that has become too difficult, they may be tempted to cut off the other person cold. You see this in the work setting as well as in families. It's very damaging to the person on the receiving end because they have no way to try to fix the relationship. And it's also damaging to the person who resorts to this tactic because they invariably cut themselves off from more and more people and become ever more isolated. They never really work through a conflict; they use cutoffs as their means to "resolve" the situation.

Cutoffs are almost never the way to go, except perhaps when there is a threat of violence. Even then, there may be a way to see the other person when others are present.

Your Reflections

- Take time out from a difficult relationship if you need a **cooling-off period**, and let the person know that you'll be in touch at some point in the future.
- **Seek therapy** if you feel it is warranted.
- Take a **look at your own behavior** and how it may be contributing to the toxic interactions.
- **Bring in a mediator** to work through the problem.
- **Keep in contact** through written communications if nothing else

Your Assignment

Consider if there is someone who you have cut off. Consider the psychological cost of that cutoff. If it feels safe, consider how you might reconnect with that person. If it doesn't feel safe, consider talking with a professional about the relationship.

CHAPTER TEN

Self-Discovery Step Seven: Define Your Mission and Core Values

Draft A Personal Mission Statement

Mission is about a very big question: What are you here on Earth to do?

It's a question most of us ponder at some point in our lives, but it's one of the most difficult to answer. Surprisingly, many successful leaders do have an answer, and in the best cases there is strong alignment between what they are leading and what they perceive as their mission.

Mission = Action:
- I am here to do something.
- I am here to act on the environment.

A mission is usually so big, it's rarely finished. It's not necessarily a goal to be achieved but more like a lifelong journey with an ending off in the distant future. It also isn't something you invent. More than likely, it's something that springs from deep inside, something you've been doing or an inclination you've had all along.

Dr. Rob's mission is to make the world a better place by helping individuals and organizations reach their full potential. That sounds vague and immeasurable. It was his mission even before he could conceptualize the notion of a mission.

When there was racial tension in the high school Dr. Rob attended, he organized other students and put together a student relations council to talk about and deal with the problems. That ability to bring people of different backgrounds together is something Dr. Rob has been dedicated to his whole life.

Have you discovered your mission yet? If so do you have a mission statement?

Your Assignment: Draft Your Personal Mission Statement

As you get ready to draft your personal mission statement, ask yourself:
- Why am I here on earth?
- What are the things that have driven me since I started high school?
- What actions have I taken to further my mission?

Here are some examples from student mission statements:
- Be the first in my family to graduate from college
- Provide for others
- Define an unmet need in society and affect it
- Teach financial literacy to kids in Detroit
- Increase opportunity and education for others
- Empower people from underprivileged groups
- Create a better life for my future family
- Be a role model to my family and underrepresented communities
- Give someone an opportunity
- Increase the number of under-represented minorities in sciences
- Support the emotional needs of underprivileged youth
- Live a fulfilling life
- Connect underprivileged youth with sports

Give Back

Who will really know why some succeed and some do not? Regardless of the circumstances, those who find themselves successful, whether by accident of birth or by their own hard work, fully distinguish themselves by giving back to the communities and societies from which they come.

To be a truly self-aware, you have to be like that farmer and put the seed back into the soil. Successful actor, Paul Newman started camps for children with serious illnesses and began a food company that gave its profits to nonprofit organizations. He was a beacon for what successful leaders can do if they focus on giving back.

We have met many leaders who are willing to give of themselves in appreciation for their success and in gratitude to society. Giving back has become more important to them than their initial success in business or industry.

They have started food-gathering organizations to collect the surplus from restaurants for the hungry. They have rebuilt some of the worst parts of the worst cities in Michigan. They have gone to Africa to help governments treat AIDS. They have adopted needy children and started projects to collect the stories of genocide survivors. They have helped the victims of Sept. 11 identify lost family members through DNA matching.

We believe this current generation of young professionals will distinguish themselves as the giving generation as they often give while they are securing a stable income or launching a career. Numerous young adults work on the presidential campaigns. All over America and throughout the world, people are making a difference by giving back.

Your Reflections

- Ask yourself: What am I doing today to give back?
- As you become more successful, what is your dream about how to give back to society?
- How will you plant the seeds today to replenish what you have been given in life?
- How will you teach your children the importance of giving back?
- What example are you setting for your children and coworkers about the importance of giving back?

Your Assignment

> Write your own statement about how you plan to give back. What inspires you. Will you give time, money, something else? By when do you plan to do this? Will you need the permission or support of others to do this?

Define Your Core Values

Your core values are the things that guide you, that you stick with no matter what. They may be as simple as, "I'm always going to tell the truth" or "I'm always going to respect others." They are the principles you abide by and vow not to compromise. Sooner or later you will be in situations where a course of action isn't clear. These values will guide your actions.

Your list of core values should include statements about what you will and will not do in conducting your life. They serve as a guide to your decision-making and attitude formation. Without core values as a guide, it is easy to lose your way personally and professionally.

Here are some examples of individual core values:
- Stay true to my faith.
- Show the love I have for the people in my life.
- Encourage people to succeed at their highest values.
- Set the right values for my company and my family, and adhere to them.
- Always tell the truth, no matter how difficult.
- Never inflict physical or emotional violence on another human being.
- Recognize the good in others.
- Always uphold my sense of integrity and adhere to my ethics.

Oprah Winfrey articulated the importance of living by your core values in these words: "Real integrity is doing the right thing, knowing that nobody's going to know whether you did it or not."

Your Assignment

> List the five core values by which you already are living your life. (If you have three or seven, that's ok).
>
> Remember, you do not have to invent your core values, you really just need to describe who you are already.
>
> Here are some tips from Dr. Vic Strecher on how to think about your core values, from his book Life on Purpose: How Living for What Matters Most Changes Everything.
> 1. Select three to five words or phrases that describe the core values that are most important to you
> 2. Think about what you would hope people would say if they were giving you a service award. What phrases might they use to describe you? What do your actions show about who you are?
>
> Add your core values to your Personal Development Plan.

CHAPTER ELEVEN

Map Your Lifestyle Values

Establishing Your Balance Points

"I arise in the morning torn between a desire to improve (or save) the world and a desire to enjoy (or savor) the world. This makes it hard to plan the day."
E.B. White

Like White, we get out of bed everyday facing a host of choices. There is no one-size-fits-all formula for how we order the day or lead our lives. Each of us must decide what will sustain us, taking into account our energy, values and passions.

The college students we talked to have an impact--and not only at work. They realize it's not enough just to have a title on the door. They want to have influence in civic life or in a faith-based or social network or movement. They want time to take care of their bodies and their souls, and they don't want to be strangers in their own homes. The challenge is to find a way, every day, to balance these arenas, even in small ways.

No matter what the setting, it's important for leaders to be in tune with those around them. You can't be a lone wolf. You can't do it all by yourself. If you try to operate without the support of the pack, you're not likely to survive. This is especially relevant for today's two-career families, where it's harder than ever to keep the home fires burning. Research shows that women still carry more than their fair share of the responsibility for child care, taking care of the extended family and handling household duties.

The most effective people are multidimensional. They're not pedal-to-the-metal types who do nothing but work for the bottom line. They're energetic and driven, but they're able to shift nimbly from one arena to the next--and that helps to establish balance points. They work intensely, and they rest intensely. They get things accomplished, but they don't expend all of their energy in one area to the detriment of others. And they don't try to do everything at once. They may not balance out every day, but they do it over time.

Here are examples of what successful people do to buoy themselves as they seek balance.

Develop Supportive Routines

We asked college students to tell us about routines that they established to help them feel more balanced.:
- *I like to prepare for the following day by laying out my clothes and packing my lunch/snacks the night before. That way when I get up in the morning, I don't need to make any of those decisions that require a lot of mental energy on my part.*
- *Yoga practice helps before bedtime - not only helps relieve pain and sore muscles but control stress. I also-induce yoga breathing before heading into a stressful situation.*
- *I need to start my day with breakfast and enough time to read the daily headlines, This helps me to feel like I took time for myself before heading into the stress and chaos of the daily grind.*

Be Realistic

- Managing our own expectations helps keep our frustration levels lower and enables us to maintain perspective until the pendulum swings back in the other direction."

Take Small Steps

- Planning guru Alan Lakein, author of *How to Get Control of Your Time and Life*, advocates using a five-minute rule if you can't seem to get started on a project. Set a timer for five minutes and work on the project. When the timer goes off, move on to something else or set the timer for another five minutes. Most people keep going for much longer than five minutes.

Examine Your Motives

- How many really get that 'less is more'? ... If our society were not driven by the constant accumulation of money, how might that change the way we live? I like money and enjoy what I can do with it, but it does not rule me.

Your Assignment

> Consider what happiness looks like to you. Write three paragraphs.
> 1. Your vision of success. Think forward to the end of your life, when you look back with satisfaction. What do you see?
> 2. Your vision of health success. What does a healthy life look like to you? What do you need to do to achieve or maintain good health?
> 3. Your vision of career success. What does career success mean to you? What do you need to do to prepare yourself for the future you seek?

Ask When Enough is Enough
- Get in the habit of comparing yourself downward as well as upward. Think about how much more you have than others.
- Travel to poorer parts of the world. It will help you appreciate what you have.
- Work at the shelter or the food bank; get close to the people it serves. Take your kids along.
- Remember where you came from. Always appreciate how far you've come--and how far you have to go.

Your Assignment

> Contemplate your relationship with symbols of success, such as material goods or status. For material things, do you take pride in quality or do you prefer to live lightly? Do you aspire to a big house, a fancy car, an exotic vacation? Do you hunger for recognition and attention?
>
> Write up your philosophy on what success means to you. How much is enough for you in possessions, in accolades or job titles.
>
> Then, think about what your family wants for you, what your friends sees as your potential. Do they match? How will you negotiate their expectations and your goals?

Balancing Act Exercise

Here is an exercise that is a precursor to setting goals, which will help you zero in on areas that need work:

1. Imagine that you are at the center of a personal ecosystem.
2. Surrounding you are five circles, symbols of the main spheres of influence in your life.
3. Now, draw a line from the SELF in the middle to each of the spheres. If the relationship is strong and there are no major issues, draw a solid line. If the relationship is strained in some way, or you feel there is unfinished business or some minor problem, draw a dotted line. If the relationship has a serious problem, draw a jagged line.

When people do this exercise honestly, they can quickly pinpoint areas where they have tension and stress. The next step is to set goals or an action plan to address the problems.

Almost anything can be resolved if you isolate the problem and set a course of action. Acting will make you feel better immediately. But if you remain in denial and do nothing, chances are the problem will eat away at you.

Your Assignment

> Draw the circles. Draw lines between the "self" and the other circles.
>
> Write up a paragraph about each connection. For instance, describe your relationship with work. Is there a solid, dotted, or jagged line? Consider why and what you will do to maintain (if positive) or fix (if strained) this relationship. Do this for all five spheres.

CHAPTER TWELVE

Defining Your Purpose

Can you define your purpose?

Dr. Rob's workshop on Visioning and Goal Setting, draws from a terrific new book, On Purpose, by his friend and University of Michigan professor, Victor Strecher. Vic wrote this graphic novel to help him rediscover life, after his family lost their 19-year-old daughter, Julia, to a rare heart disease that had plagued her since infancy.

His powerful story reinforces a truth which Rob strongly believes: for life to be meaningfully lived, we must have a purpose. Without purpose, we drift aimlessly from one activity to another with no coherent or sustained focus. Once we have defined our purpose, we will live life for a reason that transcends self and leads us towards personal growth and well-being, for self and others.

Here are some ideas on how to find your purpose:

1. Your purpose has to be **based on what you value in life**. A values clarification exercise can help you with this.
2. You need to **write down your purpose and reflect** upon it on a regular basis.
3. It's alright if **your purpose changes**, but it must grow out of careful examination of how you are living your life
4. Remember that you can have **more than one purpose**
5. Dr. Strecher also quotes Rachel Remen who said "Often, finding meaning is not about doing things differently, it is about **seeing familiar things in new ways**."

Thoughts From Ali:

In order to discover my purpose, I asked myself what I enjoy doing during my free time. I also took into account my friends and family and how they may help me achieve that purpose. Try to stay away from defining your purpose as "completing my college applications", you are only stressing and restricting yourself even further. Re-evaluate your purpose throughout life and after difficult life challenges. It'll be interesting to observe how your purpose evolves with age.

Create Your Goals

Dr. Rob recommends using a simple goal-setting method that he learned from a colleague as a young man. He writes his goals on index cards using this format:
- **What?** The specific, measurable goals that I want to achieve and the date that I set them. (No vague dreams.)
- **By when?** The date for achieving the goals. (Research shows that 90-day goals can be most effective. Longer-term ones tend to get lost; shorter-term ones come to resemble to-do lists.)
- **Why?** The reason why each goal is important. What values are central to the goals?
- **How?** The process, step by step, that I will use to achieve each goal.
- **Support?** The people I will work with to achieve each goal.

Rob likes this system because it's intuitive. It follows the questions your brain would naturally ask: What do I want to do? How fast am I going to get it done? Why do I want to do it? How will I get it done? Who will help me?

Your plan doesn't have to be hugely detailed, but you do need a plan. He has a whole box of goal cards going back to 1968. As a reminder of the goals he has set, he carries a folded-up index card in his wallet listing them. He adds and crosses off as he goes.

You can find more detailed goal-setting approaches, but this low-tech version is easy and effective. And it's easily adaptable to our microchip-driven world. Feel free to make your shoebox full of goals a digital one.

Your Assignment

> Write out the short- and long-term goals that will get you the next steps towards your lifetime vision. Define their what, by when, why, how, and describe the support you will need to achieve them.
>
> Prioritize and make a plan for each goal. Consider what might keep you from achieving these goals and make plans to address perceived obstacles. Write these out in your Personal Development Plan.

Who? Pick Your Support Team

One of the myths that people often hold dear is that they are responsible for their own success. But today, there is more and more acceptance of the notion that if you are going to succeed, it will be within a community, a group of other committed souls.

We shouldn't be surprised at this. Think about the great innovators and doers in history. Were they operating solo? Was Thomas Edison working alone in his lab? Was Michelangelo up on the scaffolding all by himself, day in and day out?

People seek out and rely on social connections to a far greater extent than they did even a few decades ago. Think about the success of online networking sites like LinkedIn and Facebook. If you accept that most things are accomplished with a "posse," it's clear that you must think about who will accompany you on your journey, who will support you and help fill in the gaps. This takes on even greater importance during bad economic times. If you lose your job, your network might help you find a new one. Isolated people have a much harder time of it. Your network needn't just be online. Yours may be your sports teams or school clubs.

Be Realistic

It's important to be realistic when you set goals--to pick things that you have some reasonable expectation and probability of achieving. You don't want to set a goal of playing basketball in the NBA when you didn't even make your high school team.

Goals also should be specific and measurable. Don't plan to change your personality or something fundamental about you; rather, it's about altering your behavior so you can reach the goal. So, focus on things that you can control. (Realize, too, that you can't control someone else's behavior, though you can control your reaction to what they do.)

The Serenity Prayer is useful to keep in mind as you set goals. What are you hoping or praying for? Are you seeking the courage to set a goal or should you be aiming for something short of that--a "serenity goal" of acceptance and the courage to deal with a problem or issue on that level?

Break down your goals into achievable steps. Your goal may be to run a marathon. The first step might be to run daily, any amount. Then, you might build up your runs to longer distances. Each step should take you closer to your ultimate goal.

And finally, when you do succeed at one of your goals, enjoy your success. Reward yourself. Buy something you've wanted. Take a trip you've been meaning to take. Do something that gives you a pat on the back and brings a smile to your face.

Your Reflection

- Review your vision and goals you have created so far. Are there ways you should edit them to make them more realistic?
- Build in a few intermediate milestones where you plan celebrations to mark your progress.
- Share them with a trusted friend or family member and ask for their feedback on them, including the realism of your timelines.

***Thoughts From Ali**:*
Setting out a list of to-do items or short-term goals and only ending up completing half of them may leave you feeling very unproductive. Which is why it's important to utilize your daily journal to complement this book. Listing reasonable priorities in your daily journal and actually being able to fulfill them won't leave you with a feeling of uneasiness. However, beware not to undermine your strengths when setting your goals. Your goals are meant to be challenging, but not to the point of impossible. Sticking to a strict daily schedule, being aware of when you're procrastinating, and being receptive to feedback will allow you to achieve your life goals.

Usually when we think of willpower, we think about resisting short term pleasure for long term gain. However, sustained willpower is what is required to achieve long term goals.

Kathleen Craig's story illustrates this principle. When she graduated from high school, Kathleen started college with the goal of achieving a bachelor's degree. However, as often is the case, life showed up. Within a few years Kathleen got married, started her family, and began a career working full time.

Although these events presented obstacles, Kathleen never lost sight of her goal to graduate. After over a decade, she returned and received her degree from EMU. Not only did she reach that goal, but she also created a new goal and launched a business. The company has created an app that helps teach financial literacy to children. Since they have already sold their product to several banks, she was recently able to give up her day job to work full time on the company.

We recently asked Kathleen how she found the willpower to keep going in the face of so many challenges. Here are a few of her keys to success:

- She kept motivated by remembering that she wanted the goal, not only for herself, but also for her children **(Find a strong motivator).**
- She never allowed herself to imagine that she would not achieve the goal **("NO" is not an option).**
- She used her willpower to stick to a strict schedule for studying, Sunday and Monday evenings and after the kids went to bed at 8:00PM **(Be disciplined in scheduling specific times to work on your goal).**
- She would only allow herself to watch TV if she studied during the commercials. Inevitably, she would get going and realize she needed to turn the TV off in order to properly focus. At least this would get her going, when all she really wanted to do was have leisure time. **(Sometimes you need to trick yourself into getting started).**

- She relied on the support of a community which included her parents, 5 brothers and sisters, and her husband. It didn't hurt that she was motivated to be the first of her siblings to graduate from college. **(It takes a community, and maybe sibling rivalry, to achieve a long-term goal).**
- She always acts now and not later, getting things done as soon as possible rather than waiting until they have to be done. **(Have a "Now List" rather than a "To Do List").**
- Wherever she worked, she made time to study and use her employer's training, mentoring, and coaching resources. **(Use the resources available and don't be afraid to ask for help).**
- The path was not continuous, but she always kept her eye on the goal. **(Hit "pause" but never "stop").**

Fear & Risk: Trust Your Gut or Do It Anyway?

During the college application process, Lauryn anxiously awaited decisions from the colleges she had applied to. She had thought she wanted to attend a more prestigious university with a great academic reputation. However, when she visited those campuses, she felt something was not right for her. She could not articulate why, but she just did not see herself on these campuses for the next four years. She had visited a university that was not previously on her radar, not at the top of the academic rankings, which she didn't think was high on her list. During the visit, she found that she immediately felt at home on this campus.

Lauryn liked everything about the latter school. It had a solid academic reputation, the location was in a city but not too urban, and there appeared to be ample opportunities for her to get involved in campus life. However, she waited to commit to this university. Over the following months, she was accepted at several other universities. She was able to narrow her choice down to two. One was the university she really liked and the other met her academic expectations but she did not like the location or size of the campus.

She experienced a lot of confusion and inability to make a decision. She decided to write down her fears. From this she learned that she felt like people would think she was foolish if she passed on the more elite university for the smaller, more comfortable university. She was able to work through her fears and decided it was more important to follow her gut and go where she felt most comfortable.

Here are the steps Lauryn took to examine her fears and make a decision:
- She examined what it was she feared, and why she was lacking confidence in this matter, even though she was generally a confident person.
- She imagined worst-case scenarios: If what she feared happened, did she believe she would be able to cope with it? Could she deal with the possibility of being judged?
- How would she feel if he passed up the opportunity and it never came around again?

- How had she been able to deal with similar decisions in the past? What inner and external resources had she called upon to enable her to face and overcome her fear?

Boost Your Resiliency Quotient

Resiliency is the ability to rebound from hardship, difficulty and misfortune and successfully adapt to adverse situations. It's perhaps more important today than ever, because the world is more interconnected than at any time in history. This interconnectedness means we experience turmoil faster, more intensely and more often.

Nothing great in life is ever achieved without taking considerable risk and facing distinct difficulties.

So, going forward, it's important to understand how you have handled adversity in the past. That's the best predictor of how you will handle it in the future.

Your Reflections

- How accurately do you assess the risks in challenging situations?
- Where would you place yourself on the cautiousness scale--over or under?
- Do you tend to be excessively optimistic or pessimistic?
- Does risk cause you to charge forward or retreat?
- Do you set realistic but challenging goals?

Tips

- Carefully decide what you can control and what you can't. Focus your energy on the former.
- Keep perspective on your ultimate goal--for example, to get a good college education to ensure you will have future career success
- Remember, there are always other solutions. Find ways to improvise and stay flexible.
- Avoid succumbing to temptations to quit, to cheat, or to exploit.
- Keep yourself inspired: read, discuss, pray; do whatever it takes.
- Look for humor, even when the situation looks bleak.
- Remember and honor your personal stories of overcoming adversity. Find time to take care of yourself on a daily basis.
- Acknowledge fear and find a way to tame it.
- Make the tough decisions and do not look back.
- Commit to overcoming adversity--to win and not to allow yourself to fail.
- Be realistically optimistic but stay grounded in reality.
- Accept responsibility for past failures but do not beat yourself up over it.
- Find a small group of people who are willing and able to support you.

- Cast off negative people.
- Define specific, winnable goals.
- Communicate the facts, no matter how bleak.

CHAPTER THIRTEEN

Personal Development Plan and "Graduation"

Personal Development Plan
Throughout the course of planning for the future, people develop and manage a growing network of high-quality relationships. Ultimately, professional success is a function of how well you manage these relationships over the long-term.

The centerpiece of this self-guided course is for you to create your own Personal Development Plan (PDP) from the exercises in this book. Your plan will articulate a meaningful professional goal and outline a plan to achieve it. It should explain what support you need from others and how you plan to get it. When you feel you've finished, we suggest taking a half hour to present this plan to someone you trust.

Your Assignment

Review your answers from the Self-Discovery Exercises in your Personal Development Plan. • For instance, what insight did you gain from the Gallup Strengths Finder exercise? How do your strengths align with your goal? What are your blind spots and how will you mitigate them?
Review your College Sweet Spot. (appendix)
Detail your vision.
Describe your goal: • What? Describe the specific, measurable goal you want to achieve. It can be a professional goal, or a personal development goal that you connect to professional success. The goal must be something you will achieve after the end of the semester, but no longer than 12 months into the future. • By when? Set a deadline for achieving your goal. Describe success in specific detail. When you achieve your goal, what will success look like? What will success feel like? • Why? Explain why this goal is important to you personally. What core values are central to this goal? What passions will you be able to engage working toward this goal? How is this goal grounded in your mission?

- How? Describe in as much detail as possible how you will achieve this goal. How do your strengths align with this goal?
- Support? "One of the myths that people of then hold dear is that they are [solely] responsible for their own success. But today, there is more and more acceptable the notion that if you are going to succeed, it will be within a community, a group of other committed individuals." What support do you need from others to achieve this goal, and how will you get it?

Your Plan of Action:
- Describe in detail the specific actions you will take to achieve your goal. You should have 3-5 specific actions. If achieving your goal requires buy-in or actions/decisions from others, then you should include an action about how you will persuade them to support you. You should present these actions in a timeline, showing when each action will be taken, as well as major milestones along the way.

Key Insights and Takeaways:
- Communicate the key insights and takeaways you had in the course of doing this assignment – about yourself, your work, etc.

Final Assignment: Commit to Action

Our Parting Thoughts for You

Thank you for participating in this process. Here's a quick summary of what we think is important and what I wish for you.

1. **Find the correct balance** between these two opposites: **accept and love yourself** as you are, yet constantly **seek ways to make yourself even better.**
2. **Beware of your negative self-talk.** You can teach yourself to "look on the sunny side of life" even if you were not raised to do so.
3. **Know your strengths** and build on them.
4. **Recognize your blind spots** and commit to being aware of them.
5. **Consider the "why."** Before thinking about your goals, think about your life mission. Think about why you are here on this earth.
6. Create a **vivid vision** for what you would like your life to look like five years from now. Make it so compelling that you can experience it through all five senses.
7. **Set specific short-term goals** that align with your mission and will move you forward toward your vision. Write each of your goals down on an index card, and then keep the cards close.

8. **For each goal answer the following questions:** By **when**? **What** is the specific goal? **Why** is it important? **How** will you go about achieving it? **Who** will support you?
9. Learn to **say your name clearly and with confidence**. When you introduce yourself, spell your first name so people will remember it. Likewise, **make a real effort to remember the names** of those you are fortunate to meet.
10. **Be kind to everyone**, especially your FRIENDS, FAMILY and TEAMMATES.
11. **Find great friends.** We are social beings. Friends will enhance your life in every way. The quality of your friendships will be the key to your happiness in life.
12. Conceive of a **dream and believe** in it. Once you have achieved it, conceive of another dream. Keep doing this throughout your life.

We believe this book will help you implement these eleven teachings, and help you feel more confident to make decisions about college and career. Additionally, you will have an edge in the college application process by knowing yourself well and relating with people more effectively. We wish you all the best.

Thoughts From Ali:
Congratulations on completing iAWARE! Remember, you are just beginning your journey to self-discovery. Your strengths and weaknesses will change along with you, so it's important to reflect upon your Personal Development Plan as often as necessary. I believe you have most of the tools for being successful in school and beyond. It's your turn now to apply what you've learned into real life, good luck! The reason we wrote this book is that our dream is to help young people in the college application and decision process.

Appendix

*Appendix 1: The Harvard Business Review - Emotional Intelligence Quiz**

How Would You Describe Yourself?

	ALWAYS	MOST OF THE TIME	FREQUENTLY	SOMETIMES	RARELY	NEVER
EMOTIONAL SELF-AWARENESS						
1 I can describe my emotions in the moment I experience them.						
2 I can describe my feelings in detail, beyond just "happy," "sad," "angry," and so on.						
3 I understand the reasons for my feelings.						
4 I understand how stress affects my mood and behavior.						
5 I understand my leadership strengths and weaknesses.						
Total per column						
Points per answer	x 5	x 4	x 3	x 2	x 1	x 0
Multiply the two rows above						
TOTAL SELF-AWARENESS SCORE *(sum of the row above)*						

*Source: https://hbr.org/2015/06/quiz-yourself-do-you-lead-with-emotional-intelligence

Appendix 1 EI Quiz

	ALWAYS	MOST OF THE TIME	FREQUENTLY	SOMETIMES	RARELY	NEVER
POSITIVE OUTLOOK						
6 I'm optimistic in the face of challenging circumstances.						
7 I focus on opportunities rather than obstacles.						
8 I see people as good and well-intentioned.						
9 I look forward to the future.						
10 I feel hopeful.						
Total per column						
Points per answer	x 5	x 4	x 3	x 2	x 1	x 0
Multiply the two rows above						
TOTAL POSITIVE OUTLOOK SCORE *(sum of the row above)*						

Appendix 1 EI Quiz

	ALWAYS	MOST OF THE TIME	FREQUENTLY	SOMETIMES	RARELY	NEVER
EMOTIONAL SELF-CONTROL						
11 I manage stress well.						
12 I'm calm in the face of pressure or emotional turmoil.						
13 I control my impulses.						
14 I use strong emotions, such as anger, fear, and joy, appropriately and for the good of others.						
15 I'm patient.						
Total per column						
Points per answer	x 5	x 4	x 3	x 2	x 1	x 0
Multiply the two rows above						
TOTAL EMOTIONAL SELF-CONTROL SCORE *(sum of the row above)*						

Appendix 1 EI Quiz

	ALWAYS	MOST OF THE TIME	FREQUENTLY	SOMETIMES	RARELY	NEVER
ADAPTABILITY						
16 I'm flexible when situations change unexpectedly.						
17 I'm adept at managing multiple, conflicting demands.						
18 I can easily adjust goals when circumstances change.						
19 I can shift my priorities quickly.						
20 I adapt easily when a situation is uncertain or ever-changing.						
Total per column						
Points per answer	x 5	x 4	x 3	x 2	x 1	x 0
Multiply the two rows above						
TOTAL ADAPTABILITY SCORE *(sum of the row above)*						

Appendix 1 EI Quiz

	ALWAYS	MOST OF THE TIME	FREQUENTLY	SOMETIMES	RARELY	NEVER
EMPATHY						
21 I strive to understand people's underlying feelings.						
22 My curiosity about others drives me to listen attentively to them.						
23 I try to understand why people behave the way they do.						
24 I readily understand others' viewpoints even when they are different from my own.						
25 I understand how other people's experiences affect their feelings, thoughts, and behavior.						
Total per column						
Points per answer	x 5	x 4	x 3	x 2	x 1	x 0
Multiply the two rows above						
TOTAL EMPATHY SCORE *(sum of the row above)*						

Appendix 1 EI Quiz

Get a Different Perspective

Keep in mind that this assessment is a self-report. It is very important to understand yourself based on how others see you as well. After you have completed the assessment. Get the opinion of some people who know you well.

1. Ask them to fill out this assessment based on what they know about you.
2. Invite them to talk with you about why they answered the way they did.
3. Ask them for feedback about what you do well and also about areas you could improve on.

Did other's assessment of you align with your assessment? Were there any surprises? Do you plan to work on anything as a result of this exercise?

Appendix 2 Personal Development Plan

Who Am I?

I. Key Strengths
1.
2.
3.
4.
5.

II. Your Interests & Passions

III. Your Personality

IV. Your Energy and Body

V. Your Mind

VI. Your Key Relationships

VII. Your Mission

VIII. Your Life Values

IX. Emotional Intelligence

X. Blindspots

What I Need to Accomplish

Next 3 Months: Education Goal	1 yr Education Goal	3 - 5 yr Education Goal
What? When? Why? How? With Whom?		
Next 3 Months: Personal Goal	**1 yr Personal Goal**	**3 - 5 yr Personal Goal**
What? When? Why? How? With Whom?		
Next 3 Months: Health Goal	**1 yr Health Goal**	**3 - 5 yr Health Goal**
What? When? Why? How? With Whom?		

Copyrights reserved by Robert Pasick, Ph.D. Rob@RobPasick.com

Appendix 3 College Sweet Spot

Passion
1. What activity brings you the most joy in your life?
   _____
   _____
   _____
2. What do you love to do so much that you would do it even if you weren't being paid for it?
   _____
   _____
   _____

Unique Talents
1. What do you do better than most everybody you know?
   _____
   _____
2. What are you succeeding at now that you have been succeeding at since you were a teenager?
   _____
   _____
3. What are you not good at?
   _____
   _____

Financial
1. Will my choices meet my expectations for financial gain
   _____
   _____

Values
1. Describe an organization that would enable you to uphold your ethics and societal values while simultaneously enabling you to maintain your desired work-family balance
   _____
   _____
   _____
   _____

Are you passionate about it?

Are you using your talents to the fullest?

Can you get paid enough for...

Does what you do align with your values & lifestyle?

Appendix 4 Journal Day 1

Top three priorities for today

1. _____
2. _____
3. _____

My Gratitudes { }

I would feel great about today if:

Take Good Care of:
Self   Others

Life Lessons Learned (L3)

Journal Day 2

Top three priorities for today

1. _____

2. _____

3. _____

My Gratitudes

I would feel great about today if:

Life Lessons Learned (L3)

Take Good Care of:
Self   Others

Journal Day 3

Top three priorities for today

1. _____
2. _____
3. _____

{ My Gratitudes }

I would feel great about today if:

Take Good Care of:
Self | Others

Life Lessons
Learned (L3)

Journal Day 4

Top three priorities for today

1. _____

2. _____

3. _____

My Gratitudes

I would feel great about today if:

Take Good Care of:
Self   Others

Life Lessons
Learned (L3)

Journal Day 5

Top three priorities for today

1. _____
2. _____
3. _____

{ My Gratitudes }

I would feel great about today if:

Life Lessons Learned (L3)

Take Good Care of:
Self | Others

Journal Day 6

Top three priorities for today

1. _____

2. _____

3. _____

My Gratitudes

I would feel great about today if:

Take Good Care of:
| Self | Others |

Life Lessons Learned (L3)

Journal Day 7

Top three priorities for today

1. _____
2. _____
3. _____

My Gratitudes

I would feel great about today if:

Life Lessons Learned (L3)

Take Good Care of:
Self | Others

Journal Day 8

Top three priorities for today

1. _____
2. _____
3. _____

My Gratitudes

I would feel great about today if:

Take Good Care of:
Self   Others

Life Lessons
Learned (L3)

Journal Day 9

Top three priorities for today

1. _____

2. _____

3. _____

My Gratitudes

I would feel great about today if:

Life Lessons Learned (L3)

Take Good Care of:
Self   Others

Journal Day 10

Top three priorities for today

1. _____

2. _____

3. _____

My Gratitudes

I would feel great about today if:

Life Lessons Learned (L3)

Take Good Care of:
Self   Others

Journal Day 11

Top three priorities for today

1. _____
2. _____
3. _____

My Gratitudes

I would feel great about today if:

Life Lessons Learned (L3)

Take Good Care of:
Self   Others

Journal Day 12

Top three priorities for today

1. _____

2. _____

3. _____

{ My Gratitudes }

I would feel great about today if:

Take Good Care of:
| Self | Others |

Life Lessons Learned (L3)

94

Journal Day 13

Top three priorities for today

1. _____
2. _____
3. _____

{ My Gratitudes }

I would feel great about today if:

Take Good Care of:
Self   Others

Life Lessons Learned (L3)

Journal Day 14

Top three priorities for today

1. _____

2. _____

3. _____

My Gratitudes { }

I would feel great about today if:

Take Good Care of:
Self   Others

Life Lessons Learned (L3)

Journal Day 15

Top three priorities for today

1. _____
2. _____
3. _____

My Gratitudes

I would feel great about today if:

Take Good Care of:
Self   Others

Life Lessons Learned (L3)

Journal Day 16

Top three priorities for today

1. _____

2. _____

3. _____

{ My Gratitudes }

I would feel great about today if:

Take Good Care of:
Self   Others

Life Lessons Learned (L3)

Journal Day 17

Top three priorities for today

1. _____
2. _____
3. _____

My Gratitudes

I would feel great about today if:

Take Good Care of:
Self | Others

Life Lessons Learned (L3)

Journal Day 18

Top three priorities for today

1. _____

2. _____

3. _____

My Gratitudes

I would feel great about today if:

Life Lessons Learned (L3)

Take Good Care of:
Self   Others

Journal Day 19

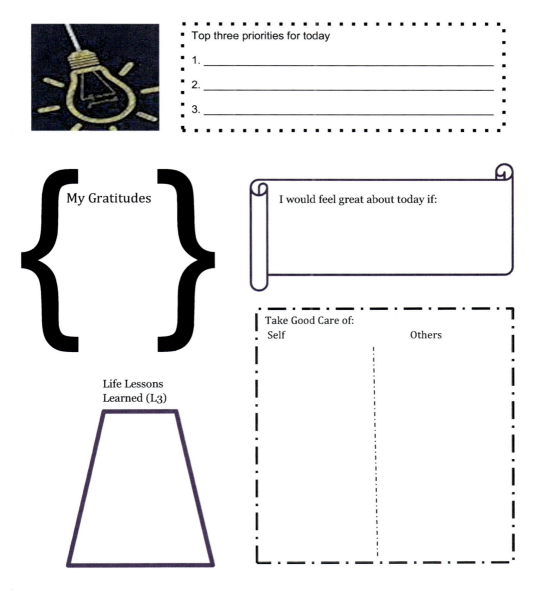

Journal Day 20

Top three priorities for today

1. _____

2. _____

3. _____

My Gratitudes

I would feel great about today if:

Take Good Care of:
Self   Others

Life Lessons
Learned (L3)

Journal Day 21

Top three priorities for today

1. _____
2. _____
3. _____

My Gratitudes { }

I would feel great about today if:

Life Lessons Learned (L3)

Take Good Care of:
Self | Others

Journal Day 22

Top three priorities for today

1. _____

2. _____

3. _____

My Gratitudes

I would feel great about today if:

Life Lessons Learned (L3)

Take Good Care of:
Self   Others

Journal Day 23

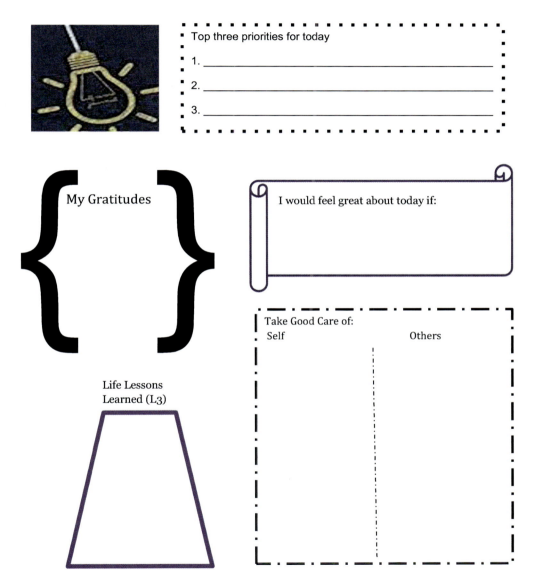

Journal Day 24

Top three priorities for today

1. _____

2. _____

3. _____

{ My Gratitudes }

I would feel great about today if:

Take Good Care of:
Self   Others

Life Lessons
Learned (L3)

Journal Day 26

Top three priorities for today

1. _____
2. _____
3. _____

My Gratitudes

I would feel great about today if:

Life Lessons Learned (L3)

Take Good Care of:
Self   Others

Journal Day 27

Top three priorities for today

1. _____
2. _____
3. _____

My Gratitudes

I would feel great about today if:

Take Good Care of:
Self   Others

Life Lessons Learned (L3)

Journal Day 28

Top three priorities for today

1. _____

2. _____

3. _____

My Gratitudes

I would feel great about today if:

Life Lessons Learned (L3)

Take Good Care of:
Self   Others

109

Journal Day 29

Top three priorities for today

1. _____

2. _____

3. _____

My Gratitudes

I would feel great about today if:

Take Good Care of:
Self   Others

Life Lessons Learned (L3)

Journal day 30

Top three priorities for today

1. _____
2. _____
3. _____

My Gratitudes

I would feel great about today if:

Take Good Care of:
Self   Others

Life Lessons
Learned (L3)

The People You Will Meet

My favorite graduation speech is not actually a speech at all. It is a delightful book written by Dr. Seuss when he was 87. It's entitled: Oh, the Places You'll Go!

Although I'm not yet 87, and I am never going to be as wise as Dr. Seuss, I'd like to share a few lines I've written as advice for graduates.

Oy, The People You Will Meet.
Congratulations, today is your graduation day,
Over the next few years you'll meet some fascinating people along the way.

Happy or sad you can choose to be,
It's the quality of the relationships that will set you free,

Some people will be interesting,
Some will be nice,
Some will treat you cold as ice.

Some people you'll meet will love to compete,
Don't be scared!
It's them you can defeat.

Some will become friends,
You can learn to get along great,
Nothing better than to collaborate.

Some will have so many ideas,
They will drive you nuts.
Others will cherish the rules
And refuse to accept any
"Ifs, ands, or buts."

So get out there and meet every type!
But beware of the ones with too much hype --
Or who blame you for their lousy state,
Or who want to get high with you on the very first date.

Or who dare you to do things, cause "you'll never get caught"
Or who shame you and make you feel like toxic waste...
You get the point, the ones who leave you with a bad taste.

So next time you're in a coffee shop or bar,
Put that phone down and look around.
Say "Hello!" with a smile --
Your future best bud might have just walked in from afar.

Acknowledgements

Lauryn and Ali would like to thank their families for support while writing this book and going through the college process with them. They are grateful to have you in their corner, providing unconditional love.

Dr. Rob, Lauryn, and Ali would also like to acknowledge and thank their peers and the college students who shared their stories and gave invaluable advice to include in this book.

Resources

Auerbach, Randy, *WHO World Health Surveys International College Student Survey: Prevalence and Distribution of Mental Disorders.* Journal of Abnormal Psychology, 2018, Vol 127, No. 7

Bradberry, Travis and Jean Greaves. *Emotional Intelligence 2.0.* San Diego, CA: TalentSmart. 2009.

Buckingham, Marcus and Donald Clifton. *Now Discover Your Strengths.* New York: Gallup Press. 2001.

Collins, Jim. *Good to Great: Why Some Companies Make the Leap ... and Others Don't.* New York: HarperCollins. 2001.

Goleman, Daniel; Richard Boyatzis and Annie McKee. *Primal Leadership: Learning to Lead with Emotional Intelligence.* Boston: Harvard Business School Press. 2004.

Gottman, John and Nan Silver. *The Seven Principles for Making Marriage Work.* New York: Three Rivers Press. 1999.

Isay, David. *Listening Is an Act of Love: A Celebration of American Life from the StoryCorps Project.* New York: Penguin Press. 2007.

Lakein, Alan. *How to Get Control of Your Time and Life.* New York: Signet. 1974.

New York Times. *Portraits: 9/11/01.* New York: Times Books. 2002.

Pasick, Robert. *Awakening from the Deep Sleep: A Powerful Guide for Courageous Men.* New York: Harper Collins. 1992.

Pasick, Robert. *Conversations with My Old Dog.* Canton, Michigan: David Crumm Media, LLC. 2009.

Pasick, Robert. *Balanced Leadership in Unbalanced Times.* Canton, Michigan: David Crumm Media, LLC. 2009.

Pausch, Randy with Jeffrey Zaslow. *The Last Lecture.* New York: Hyperion. 2008.

Quinn, Robert E. *Building the Bridge As You Walk On It: A Guide for Leading Change.* San Francisco: Jossey-Bass. 1996.

Quinn, Robert E. *Deep Change: Discovering the Leader Within.* San Francisco: Jossey-Bass. 1996.

Rath, Tom. *StrengthsFinder 2.0.* New York: Gallup Press. 2007.

Rath, Tom and Donald O. Clifton. *How Full Is Your Bucket? Positive Strategies for Work and Life.* New York: Gallup Press. 2004.

Strecher, Vic. *Life on Purpose: How Living for What Matters Most Changes Everything.* New York: Harper Collins. 2016.

Weinzweig, Ari. *Zingerman's Guide to Good Leading, Part Three: A Lapsed Anarchist's Approach to Managing Ourselves.* Ann Arbor, Michigan: Zingerman's Press. 2013.

Weinzweig, Ari. *Zingerman's Guide to Good Leading, Part Four: A Lapsed Anarchist's Approach to the Power of Beliefs in Business.* Ann Arbor, Michigan: Zingerman's Press. 2016.

Authors

Rob Pasick, Ph.D.

"Dr. Rob" is an Executive Coach, Organizational Psychologist, and a Lecturer at the University of Michigan Ross School of Business and at the University of Michigan's Center for Entrepreneurship at the College of Engineering.
Rob has been practicing in the Ann Arbor area as a Clinical & Organizational Psychologist and Executive Coach since he earned his Ph.D. from Harvard University in 1975.
Rob has appeared on "Oprah" and "The Today Show." He is the founder and host of Leaders Connect, which provides monthly Leaders Connect Breakfast networking events and Leadership Roundtables to the community.

Lauryn Humphreys

Lauryn is a senior at Saline High School, in Saline, Michigan, where she is active on student council, key club, debate and dance team. She also figure skates for Findlay Silver Blades Figure Skating Club, and is a member of the competitive synchronized skating team. Lauryn plans to attend college in the fall of 2019 and major in Biomedical Engineering.

Ali Houmani

Ali is a senior at Pioneer High School in Ann Arbor, Michigan. He is a 2-year varsity soccer captain, member of the UNICEF club, and volunteer tutor. Outside of school he plays soccer for the Michigan Wolves Midwest Regional team. Ali plans on attending college in 2019 to study Biology and Finance on a pre-med track.

Made in the USA
Lexington, KY
10 June 2019